Passion Caipirinha

Pizza c̄ Onions & Smoked

Smoked Salmon on P

Chicken Soup / Matzah

Zittcug

Short ribs

Grilled Chicken c̄

Tomatoes

Sautéed Cherry Tomatoes

Veg Mash

Ret Veg

mark
mark

eigh
ennie

sley
nathan
ichard

na
dney
ncesca
inoch

App
tcho
Ch

Tom

Caesar Salad

friday night
DINNERS
bonnie stern

Photography by Mark Rupert

RANDOM HOUSE CANADA

LIBRARY AND ARCHIVES CANADA CATALOGUING IN PUBLICATION

Stern, Bonnie
    Friday night dinners / Bonnie Stern.

ISBN 978-0-307-35675-8

    1. Dinners and dining. 2. Menus. I. Title.
TX714.B853 2008   641.5'4   C2008-901662-9

Photography: Mark Rupert
Project Editor: Shelley Tanaka

Photos of Mark Rupert, courtesy Anna Rupert
Photo p. 192 courtesy Corporal Joe Mousseau
All other photos courtesy the author

Jacket and text design: CS Richardson

Printed and bound in China

10 9 8 7 6 5 4 3 2 1

For Ruthie and Maxie, who instilled in me a love of family— what I wouldn't give to have one more Friday night dinner with you.

And for Ray, Mark, Anna and Fara, who remind me every week why I love Friday night dinners so much.

contents

acknowledgments

This book is about family, but not just the traditional idea of family. Everyone has different groups of people—friends and associates from work, hobbies, clubs, sports and volunteer activities who make up little families around them—and I am lucky to have many people in my life who provide inspiration and support.

My immediate family—Ray, my partner in Friday night dinners and everything else, and Mark, Anna and Fara, whom I trust to carry on the tradition of Friday night dinners.

My sister, Jane, and her family—Wayne, Meredith, Chuck and Adam—my sister-in-law, Heddy, the Soltz family and the Stern family.

The FND regulars—those who help with the dishes and everyone who "taste tests" my recipes—Leslie Milrod and Jonathan Guss; Lauren, Jan, Daniel and Adam Gutter; Patti, Joey and Earl Linzon; Mark Moors; Jonathan Born; Richard Rotman; Hanoch Drori; Rob Dittmer; Sydney Bacon and Francesca Horbay; Lynn Saunders; Anita Ivanauskus and Mike Gravelle; Marsha Werb and Ed Hamer; Janice Zolf; Andrea Iceruk; Maureen Lollar; Bernie Glazman; Irene Tam; Beth Landau-Halpern; Susan and John Devins; Julia Sharp; Katie Coristine; Eric and Helen Kirzner; Ann Sharp and Vernon Shaw; Nathan Goldstein; Harvey and Bev Botting; Klaus Tenter and Liz Addison; Richard Lewin and Myra Sourkes.

My friends and mentors Rabbi Elyse Goldstein, who always seems to know the right thing to do in every situation and who, through our trips to Israel, has enhanced my Friday night dinners forever; Mildred Istona, who encouraged me to write a personal book about something I am passionate about; Judy Stacey Goldman, my "sister" in Israel; Gwen Berkowitz, one of the best cooks I have ever known; Mitchell Davis, my personal encyclopedia of anything and everything relating to food and good taste; and my teachers at George Brown College, who guided me into the world of food long before it was the next big thing.

My cooking school family—Dely Balagtas, Jenny Burke, Leonie Eidinger, Jennifer Mahoney, Lorraine Butler, Lauren Gutter and Letty Lastima, who make it fun to come to work and who often become entangled in my Friday night dinners; plus Linda Stephen, Fran Berkoff, Alex Beauregard, Anne Apps, Francine Ménard, Marilia Mota, Jordan Exton, Anthony Rose, Stephen Alexander, Nathan Pond, Jerry Meneses, Rosa and Tony Marinuzzi, Hart Melvin, Jacques Marie, Rick Blackwell, David Cohlmeyer, Ruth Klahsen, Winnie and Wilson Shao, Peter and Aurora Kashkarian, and all the cooking teachers and authors we host and the suppliers who make it possible for us to have the best ingredients.

My Random House family—Anne Collins, Marlene Fraser, Janine Laporte, Brad Martin, Pamela Murray, John Neale, Ruth Pincoe, Scott Richardson, Andrew Roberts, Jennifer Shepherd and Olga Truchan—who have done such a great job producing and supporting my books. And Marian Hebb, Scott Sellers and Shelley Tanaka, who have become part of all my families, personal as well as professional, and without whom I couldn't imagine writing a book. My son, Mark Rupert, is now also part of my cookbook family, after taking hundreds (maybe thousands) of photos for this book before our real Friday night dinners (no matter how hungry he was).

My food community family has grown so much since I opened my school. In the beginning there were only a few of us, but we are now a big family of chefs, food writers, teachers, broadcasters and PR people—all promoting food as a serious career choice as well as a pleasure. Thanks for your continuing inspiration and support.

Sarah Murdoch, Deb Aldcorn, Sheilagh McEvenue, Tyler Anderson, Peter Thompson, Peter Redman and Glenn Lowson of the *National Post*.

Krishan Mehta, Rick Halpern, David Clandfield, Barbara Dick and Sabrina Chang at the University of Toronto, who brought me back to the university family.

My Sherritt family—Jowdat Waheed, Ian Delaney, Liz Baston and Himalaya Rana—who have given me the opportunity to work with and coach their chefs (Oday, Kindelin and Damien).

Finally, my family of students—after all these years of teaching cooking classes, I trust you to tell me what you need to know to cook my recipes, and I trust you to continue the tradition of family dinners. I am honored that you welcome me into your homes by cooking my recipes.

introduction

Friday night dinner means different things to different people, but to anyone who is Jewish, it means a special family dinner to celebrate the end of the work week and to welcome Shabbat, the day of rest. It is a wonderful tradition that everyone can enjoy.

Whether Jewish people are religious or not, whether they are kosher or not, whether they observe Shabbat or not, most know about Friday night dinner. When my sister and I were growing up (even though our family was not religious or kosher or very observant), my mom always made Friday night dinner, and although she didn't make us come (the way some of our friends' parents did) we nearly always made our plans so that we could be with the family on Friday nights. She would often invite our friends or their friends—our house was always full.

After my parents died, Friday night dinner was even more important to me. It became a time to reminisce about Ruthie and Maxie, use my mother's dishes, discuss the week that had gone by with the kids, invite people over and just relax.

Even if you are not Jewish, Friday night is a perfect time to share a meal with family and friends. When you entertain on Saturday night, there is often an expectation of an elaborate, impressive and maybe even formal dinner, whether on the part of guests or the host. When you entertain on Sunday night, people are starting to get anxious about the week ahead and are expecting (or hoping for!) an early night. But Friday night is the ideal time to relax after a week of work. A recent article in the London *Observer* reported that with weekends now filled with work, shopping and other activities, Friday evenings have replaced Sunday lunch as the time when many modern families get together over a meal.

When you invite people to a Friday night family dinner, guests will usually offer to help you cook, set the table and even clean up. Let them! I used to think everything had to be perfect when guests came over, but I have found that people appreciate and feel honored to be part of the family more than anything else.

The idea for this book developed from the dinner diary I have kept for the past twenty-six years. It includes all the menus, and the names of the guests who have come over for dinner since Ray and I were married. When I look back through the diaries I am reminded how far back so many friendships go, and I can see all of our children's milestones. I can see that when Mark was born it took me ten hours to cook a dinner that would normally take me an hour to prepare. I can see that after Anna was born I didn't invite anyone over for months (having two kids turned out to keep me much busier than I'd expected!). I can see when Ray's daughter Fara came to live with us, and all the kids' friends who came to dinner along the way. I can see when I was making the same things over and over (everyone goes on kicks, even me), how my cooking style has changed (no more formal multicourse meals or dependency on butter and cream) and which recipes (gougères, Caesar salad, guacamole and lemon pudding cake) have come back in style (either the same or updated) after many years. I can also see how I've recreated recipes after returning home from various trips, and why Ray and the kids would tease me that our house had turned into Bonnie's Chinese Bistro, Bonnie's Vietnamese Bistro, Bonnie's South African Bistro, etc.

Saying goodbye to the work week and hello to the weekend is a good reason for anyone to have Friday night dinner. And there are many ways to cook it. The menus in this book cover the gamut of quick meals, meals from different countries, vegetarian meals, seasonal, holiday, comfort and everything that I (and I hope you, too) like to cook for those I love. And in respect for the Jewish tradition of Friday night dinners, the recipes and menus in this book are kosher friendly.

Most people work, so coming home at five and hosting a dinner party requires some planning. My family will tell you that for the first half hour I am really bossy, and everyone stays out of my way. But then I make a plan and calm down, everyone shows up to help, and everything falls into place. Although I sometimes put together a meal at the last minute (see the Fast Food menus for suggestions), planning and preparing a few things ahead can really take the pressure off (see the introductions to each menu for make-ahead suggestions).

I serve dinner in a casual family style, because I like to know I'm eating at home, not in a restaurant. I rarely serve plated dishes. Instead we usually offer guests drinks (that's Ray's job) and appetizers when they arrive (sometimes I even serve soup as a pre-dinner appetizer in little shooter glasses or tea cups) and then sit down to the main course with me serving from platters at the table.

In many ways, the preparation of this book has been a family affair. This really is a reality cookbook. My son, Mark, took the photographs, Anna would often be my sous chef or Mark's photography assistant, and the whole family helped with everything from preparing the recipes to setting up for the photos to evaluating the menus. When we needed to shoot more photos, our dinners sometimes included dishes from more than one menu, and guests would look at the array of food on the table and ask Ray, "Do you always eat like this?" And everyone got used to the line, "Oops, don't eat that! We need to take the photo first!"

Like most passionate cooks, I sometimes give you too much—too much food, too many recipes, too many tips. But remember that you don't have to make everything, and you can mix and match to create your own menus. Many of the appetizers can be converted to main courses, many of the salads can be served as a first course, and you can adjust quantities to suit the number of people you are cooking for. Servings are relatively large because I always think it is better to have more than not enough, but I love leftovers and there are suggestions for those, too. If you are knowledgable about wine, you'll be able to choose the wine yourself to match the menu you're preparing, but if you need a recommendation, take the recipes to your local wine store and ask the consultant to suggest something that is within your price range.

A lot has been said about people not cooking these days, because we are eating in restaurants and buying take-out food more often. But where has that led us? No one even knows what is in their food anymore. People eat all kinds of processed foods, and yet they are afraid of a piece of homemade chocolate cake. Most of the recipes in this book are very healthful, but I do think that Friday night dinner is a time to indulge yourself a little. Not only will the food you make be of better quality than anything you buy, but it will have been cooked by you for the people you care about.

Recently when Ray and I were in Israel, Anna and Fara got together back at home and made an amazing Friday night dinner for family and friends. They said it was quite a bit of work (they made the laid-back turkey, stuffing, mashed potatoes, salad and chocolate cake), but they also discovered that cooking is easy and fun. And they got to experience first hand what it felt like to work together, feed others and feel appreciated.

If you don't want to cook a full meal, potluck Friday night dinner is also a good solution. Offer your house as the venue, make the main course and suggest easy things for guests to bring. One person can bring salad and another can make mashed potatoes. Others can bring a fruit tray or cookies. People who don't want to cook can bring wine, bread or flowers—it doesn't really matter, as long as they come and feel part of it.

With this book I hope to convince you that Friday night is the perfect time to have a family meal, whether that includes your immediate family, relatives or an extended family of friends, business associates and coworkers.

One more thing. We have just added a new tradition when we sit down to Friday night dinner. When Ray and I were in Jerusalem at Friday night services at Kol HaNeshama, Rabbi Levi Weiman-Kellman suggested a wonderful way to close the week. He asked everyone to take a deep breath and think about the week gone by . . . and then to breathe out to let it go and say goodbye.

Try it.

Bonnie Stern

HUMMOS WITH CILANTRO PESTO
GRILLED PITA WITH ZA'ATAR
SHORTRIBS WITH RED WINE AND PORT
BUTTERNUT RIBBONS
SMASHED RED-SKINNED POTATOES
MIXED GREENS WITH MUSTARD TARRAGON DRESSING
LEMON MERINGUE PIE

comfort dinner

SERVES 8

Friday night dinners are all about enjoying a good meal with family and friends in a relaxed and comfortable atmosphere. Shortribs, mashed potatoes and lemon meringue pie are a few of my family's all-time favorites, and for me they make up the ultimate comfort meal.

Make the shortribs ahead and freeze them or, better yet, double the recipe and freeze half for another time. Leftovers can be used as a topping for pasta, in shepherd's pie (page 89) or ravioli, or with mashed potatoes in pierogi (page 90).

The pie, shortribs, salad dressing and hummos can all be made ahead. Reheat the shortribs while the squash and potatoes are cooking. The pita can be served at room temperature or grilled just before serving.

Hummos with Cilantro Pesto

If you think hummos is old hat, try this. It is a staple at my Friday night dinners. My good friend Hanoch Drori inspired this recipe, but there are many variations. Extra pesto can be used to garnish soups or pastas; it is also perfect in guacamole. Use your favorite basil pesto, matboucha (page 100) or salsa verde (page 288) instead of the cilantro pesto if you wish.

HUMMOS
2 cups (500 mL) cooked or canned chickpeas
2 cloves garlic, chopped
⅓ cup (75 mL) tahina
3 tbsp (45 mL) lemon juice
3 tbsp (45 mL) extra-virgin olive oil
½ tsp (2 mL) ground cumin (preferably toasted)
1 tsp (5 mL) kosher salt
3 tbsp (45 mL) water or unflavored yogurt, approx.
¼ tsp (1 mL) hot red pepper sauce

CILANTRO PESTO (Z'HOUG)
2 cloves garlic, peeled
1 jalapeño, coarsely chopped (or to taste)
1 cup (250 mL) packed fresh cilantro
½ tsp (2 mL) kosher salt
⅓ cup (75 mL) extra-virgin olive oil

1. To prepare hummos, reserve 2 tbsp (25 mL) chickpeas for a garnish. In a food processor, puree remaining chickpeas with garlic, tahina, lemon juice, oil, cumin and salt. Add enough water to make a smooth and creamy spread. Season with hot pepper sauce. Taste and adjust seasonings if necessary.
2. Spread hummos over center of a serving plate and sprinkle with reserved chickpeas.
3. For cilantro pesto, chop garlic and jalapeño in a food processor. Add cilantro and puree. Blend in salt and oil.
4. Drizzle about half the pesto around edge of hummos and over surface. (Freeze remainder.)

MAKES 2 CUPS (500 ML)

Grilled Pita with Za'atar

Za'atar refers to two things—a herb (hyssop) and, more commonly, a Middle Eastern blend of herbs and spices that includes thyme, sesame seeds and sumac. At a spice store in Israel I saw at least ten mounds of za'atar from different countries, and each one looked and tasted unique. It is available at Middle Eastern markets and is great on chicken, salmon or lamb.

4 6-inch (15 cm) pita breads
2 tbsp (25 mL) extra-virgin olive oil
2 tbsp (25 mL) za'atar or dried thyme
1 tsp (5 mL) sea salt (e.g., Maldon)

1. Brush one side of each pita with oil and sprinkle with za'atar and salt.
2. Grill pitas until lightly browned, about 1 to 2 minutes per side (I usually grill the oiled side first). Cut into wedges.

Guacamole with Cilantro Pesto
Mash a ripe avocado and combine with 1 tbsp (15 mL) lime juice and 2 tbsp (25 mL) cilantro pesto.

Makes about ¾ cup (175 mL).

Ricotta and Cilantro Pesto Dip
Combine 1 cup (250 mL) ricotta cheese with 2 tbsp (25 mL) cilantro pesto.

Makes about 1 cup (250 mL).

Hummos Pancakes
This is a great way to use leftover hummos. Serve the pancakes as an appetizer or snack with date honey (page 72) or hot red pepper jelly.

In a food processor, combine 1 cup (250 mL) hummos, 2 eggs, ¼ cup (50 mL) all-purpose or whole wheat flour, ½ tsp (2 mL) ground cumin and 2 tbsp (25 mL) chopped fresh cilantro.

In a large skillet, heat 2 tbsp (25 mL) extra-virgin olive oil over medium-high heat. Drop batter by scant tablespoon into pan. Cook for about 2 minutes per side.

Makes 20 to 24 2-inch (5 cm) pancakes.

Shortribs with Red Wine and Port

Shortribs are sold many different ways, so they can be a bit confusing, but it is worth figuring them out. They are a tough cut and can only be cooked quickly if they are cut very thinly, as with Miami ribs (page 250). For braised recipes like this one, they are usually cut in 2- to 3-inch (5 to 7.5 cm) chunks or in long, thick pieces and cooked for a long time.

8 lb (4 kg) shortribs, cut lengthwise or in large chunks
Salt and pepper to taste
2 tbsp (25 mL) extra-virgin olive oil
2 large onions, chopped
4 cloves garlic, finely chopped
2 carrots, diced
1 cup (250 mL) Port or dry red wine
3 sprigs fresh thyme
2 cups (500 mL) dry red wine
2 cups (500 mL) beef stock, chicken stock or water
½ cup (125 mL) demi glace, optional
2 tbsp (25 mL) chopped fresh parsley

1. Pat shortribs dry and season generously with salt and pepper.
2. Heat oil in a large Dutch oven over medium-high heat. Add shortribs in batches and brown well on all sides. (This will take about 10 to 15 minutes.) Remove meat from pan.
3. Discard all but 2 tbsp (25 mL) fat from pan. Add onions, garlic and carrots. Cook until slightly browned and tender, about 10 minutes.
4. Add Port and thyme. Cook for 5 minutes, or until reduced to ¼ cup (50 mL).
5. Add wine, bring to a boil and cook for 5 minutes. Add stock and demi glace, if using.
6. Return shortribs to pan. Liquid should come halfway up sides of meat. Cover shortribs with parchment paper and then with a tight lid or heavy foil.
7. Cook shortribs in a preheated 350°F (180°C) oven for at least 2½ to 3 hours or longer, or until meltingly tender. Remove meat from pan.
8. Strain juices and remove fat. If juices have not reduced enough, boil on stove until you have about 2 cups (500 mL). Add shortribs and reheat thoroughly. Serve sprinkled with parsley.

MAKES 8 SERVINGS

Jenny's Asian-flavored Shortribs

Jenny Cheng Burke, who works with me at the cooking school, developed this version of shortribs when Jan Wong (author of *Beijing Confidential*) was guest of honor at our book club.

Season shortribs with salt, pepper and ½ tsp (2 mL) five-spice powder. Brown shortribs and remove from pan.

Add 1 bunch green onions, 4 chopped cloves garlic, 2 tbsp (25 mL) chopped fresh ginger and ¼ tsp (1 mL) hot red pepper flakes to pan. Cook for a few minutes.

Add 2 tbsp (25 mL) brown sugar, 5 star anise, 2 tbsp (25 mL) Szechwan peppercorns, 1 bunch fresh cilantro, ⅓ cup (75 mL) sake, 3 tbsp (45 mL) soy sauce, ½ cup (125 mL) orange juice and 4 cups (1 L) beef stock or water. Bring to a boil.

Return shortribs to pan and proceed as in Step 6.

When shortribs are cooked, remove from pan. Strain sauce and reduce to about 2 cups (500 mL). Add 2 lb (1 kg) peeled daikon radish cut in sticks. Simmer, covered, for 30 minutes. Return shortribs to pan and reheat thoroughly.

Serve garnished with fresh cilantro.

Butternut Ribbons

These thin strips of butternut look like wide noodles or ribbons. They taste delicious and make a wonderful vegetable garnish. Buy peeled squash or peel the squash yourself with a vegetable peeler. (You can even leave the peel on and eat it!)

> 3 lb (1.5 kg) butternut squash
> 2 tbsp (25 mL) extra-virgin olive oil
> 1 tsp (5 mL) kosher salt
> 1 tbsp (15 mL) chopped fresh thyme or rosemary, or ½ tsp (2 mL) dried

1. Cut squash into strips about ⅛ inch (3 mm) thick, 4 inches (10 cm) long and 1 inch (2.5 cm) wide. Arrange on parchment-lined baking sheets in a single layer.
2. Sprinkle or brush with oil and sprinkle with salt and thyme.
3. Roast in a preheated 400°F (200°C) for 25 to 35 minutes, or until browned.

MAKES 8 SERVINGS

Smashed Red-skinned Potatoes

When my kids were little, smooth and creamy was the only way to go when it came to mashed potatoes, but now we are much more flexible. These smashed potatoes go well with any saucy, stewed or braised dish, or topped with steak or lamb chops. You can also add a couple of spoonfuls of caramelized onions.

3 lb (1.5 kg) red-skinned potatoes, unpeeled and cut in chunks
1 head roasted garlic (page 173)
¼ cup (50 mL) extra-virgin olive oil or butter (or to taste)
2 tsp (10 mL) kosher salt
¼ tsp (1 mL) pepper
2 tbsp (25 mL) chopped fresh parsley

1. In a large pot, cover potatoes with plenty of salted water and bring to a boil. Reduce heat and simmer for 20 to 25 minutes, or until tender.
2. Drain potatoes and return to pan, saving about ½ cup (125 mL) cooking liquid. Squeeze garlic out of skins and add to potatoes along with oil, salt and pepper. With a potato masher, mash coarsely. (If potatoes are too thick, add a little hot potato-cooking liquid, stock or milk.) Add parsley. Taste and adjust seasonings if necessary.

MAKES 8 SERVINGS

Mixed Greens with Mustard Tarragon Dressing

Use just enough dressing to coat the greens. Extra dressing will keep in the refrigerator for at least five days. If you want the dressing to be a little sweeter, add more honey.

Because good red wine vinegar can be hard to find, I often use sherry vinegar instead.

2 tbsp (25 mL) sherry vinegar
1 tsp (5 mL) honey
1 tsp (5 mL) Dijon mustard
1 tsp (5 mL) kosher salt
1 clove garlic, minced
1 tbsp (15 mL) chopped fresh tarragon
½ cup (125 mL) extra-virgin olive oil
12 cups (3 L) mixed greens

1. In a small bowl, whisk vinegar, honey, mustard, salt, garlic and tarragon.
2. Drizzle in oil while whisking. Taste and adjust seasonings if necessary.
3. Place mixed greens in a large bowl. Add dressing to taste and toss before serving.

MAKES 8 SERVINGS

Lemon Meringue Pie

My mother often made lemon meringue pie. When I was little she used to make the crust by hand, but when my sister was born, she started buying frozen pie crust. I remember thinking that meant she must love me more, but later when I confronted her she laughed and said that when I was little you couldn't buy frozen crust.

You can swirl the meringue or pipe it in mounds or rosettes.

1 cup (250 mL) all-purpose flour
Pinch kosher salt
½ cup (125 mL) butter or margarine, cold, cut in pieces
4 tbsp (50 mL) ice water, approx.

FILLING
1 cup (250 mL) lemon juice
1¼ cups (300 mL) granulated sugar
3 eggs
3 egg yolks
¼ cup (50 mL) butter or margarine, cold, cut in pieces
1 tbsp (15 mL) grated lemon peel

MERINGUE
3 egg whites
¾ cup (175 mL) granulated sugar

1. For pastry, in a bowl or food processor, combine flour and salt. Cut in butter until it is in tiny bits. Sprinkle with ice water and knead together into a ball. Wrap in plastic wrap and refrigerate for 30 minutes.

2. On a floured board, roll out dough to fit a 9-inch (23 cm) tart pan with removable bottom. Press dough into pan and double over sides. (Or fit pastry into a shallow 9-inch/23 cm regular pie dish and fold over edges to crimp.)

3. Line pastry shell with parchment, fill with beans, rice, pie weights or clean pennies and bake in a preheated 425°F (220°C) oven for 15 minutes. Remove weights and paper and reduce oven temperature to 375°F (190°C). Return pastry to oven and bake for 10 to 15 minutes, or until lightly browned.

4. Meanwhile, for filling, combine lemon juice and sugar in a saucepan and bring to a boil. Stir well.

5. Beat eggs and yolks in a large bowl and whisk in hot sugar mixture. Return to saucepan and cook over medium-high heat until thick. Stir in butter until melted.

6. Strain mixture and add lemon peel. Pour into tart shell and return to oven for at least 15 to 20 minutes, or until set. Cool completely.

7. For meringue, beat egg whites until frothy and white. Gradually add sugar and continue to beat until stiff.

8. Spread or pipe meringue on cooled pie. With a mini blowtorch, brown meringue. Chill if not serving right away. (Or put pie in a preheated 350°F/180°C oven for about 15 to 20 minutes to brown.)

MAKES ONE 10-INCH (25 CM) PIE

italian dinner

SERVES 6

O f all the cuisines I love, I find Italian the easiest and most user-friendly. You use fresh ingredients and don't do much to them.

This is a very adaptable menu. The chicken breasts can be served as a main course on or off the skewers, or you can replace the chicken with shrimp. The polenta can be served as an appetizer, or you can cut it into sticks to make polenta fries.

The martini base, biscotti, tomatoes, peaches and polenta can all be made ahead. Grill the chicken, endive and veal while the polenta is browning in the oven (you can also brown the veal chops ahead on the grill and finish them in the oven while the polenta is browning).

Lemon Basil Martinis

A new trend in cocktails is syrups and infusions, and this is one of my current favorites. I got the idea from A Voce, a wonderful Italian restaurant in New York. For a non-alcoholic version, use soda water instead of vodka.

> 1 cup (250 mL) water
> 1 cup (250 mL) granulated sugar
> 1 bunch fresh basil
> 1 cup (250 mL) lemon juice
> 1½ cups (375 mL) vodka
> Ice

1. In a saucepan, bring water and sugar to a boil. Add basil, reduce heat and simmer for about 5 minutes. Strain syrup and chill.
2. Combine syrup, lemon juice and vodka in a large pitcher and chill.
3. Serve (about ⅓ cup/75 mL each) in martini glasses with ice.

MAKES 6 TO 8 DRINKS

Grilled Chicken Skewers with Rosemary and Garlic

To prevent skewers from burning up on the grill, I grill the chicken breasts or thighs whole, before cutting them into strips and threading them on skewers for presentation.

> 4 boneless, skinless chicken breasts or thighs
> 2 tbsp (25 mL) extra-virgin olive oil
> 2 cloves garlic, minced
> Pinch hot red pepper flakes
> 1 ½ tsp (7 mL) kosher salt
> ½ tsp (2 mL) pepper
> 1 tbsp (15 mL) chopped fresh rosemary, or ¼ tsp (1 mL) dried
> 1 tbsp (15 mL) grated lemon peel

1. Remove filets from chicken breasts. Pound chicken breasts to even thickness. Place filets and breasts in a shallow dish.
2. In a small bowl, combine oil, garlic, hot pepper flakes, salt, pepper, rosemary and lemon peel. Rub into chicken. Marinate for up to 2 hours in refrigerator.
3. Grill chicken for 4 to 6 minutes per side, or until just cooked through (cook thighs for 8 to 10 minutes per side). Do not overcook. Cut each piece into 4 or 5 strips and thread on bamboo skewers.

MAKES 16 TO 24 APPETIZERS

Porcini-rubbed Grilled Veal Chops

I was first served these veal chops with porcini "dust" by my friend Susan Devins, a great cook and host.

Big, thick veal chops really make a statement. They are impressive, but fairly expensive, so take care to cook them properly. Make porcini powder by grinding dried porcini mushrooms in an electric spice grinder or coffee grinder until fine. If you have truffle salt, sprinkle the veal chops with a little before or after grilling.

> 6 veal chops, 1½ inches (4 cm) thick, trimmed
> 3 tbsp (45 mL) extra-virgin olive oil
> ¼ cup (50 mL) ground dried porcini mushrooms
> 2 tbsp (25 mL) granulated sugar
> 1 tbsp (15 mL) kosher salt
> 1 tsp (5 mL) dry mustard
> 1 tsp (5 mL) garlic powder
> ½ tsp (2 mL) pepper

1. Place veal chops in a single layer on a rimmed baking sheet.
2. In a small bowl, combine oil, ground mushrooms, sugar, salt, mustard, garlic powder and pepper. Rub into both sides of veal chops. If you have time, marinate for 2 to 4 hours in refrigerator.
3. Cook chops on a barbecue over high heat for 3 minutes per side. Reduce heat to medium (or move chops to side of grill) and cook for 3 minutes longer on each side, or until meat is pink but not raw inside (a meat thermometer should read 145°F/63°C). You can also grill chops for 3 minutes per side over high heat and transfer to a parchment-lined baking sheet. Roast in a preheated 400°F (200°C) oven for 10 to 15 minutes. (Or brown chops in a grill pan, in batches, before transferring to oven.)

MAKES 6 SERVINGS

Roasted Butternut Polenta

Vegetable purees add lots of flavor and color to polenta. Try 1 cup (250 mL) pureed roasted red peppers or 2 cups (500 mL) pureed cooked carrots instead of the squash.

This recipe makes lots of polenta; use some to make polenta fries. Cut the cold polenta into thick sticks about ½ inch (1 cm) wide and 3 inches (7.5 cm) long and arrange on a parchment-lined baking sheet in a single layer. Drizzle with olive oil and roast in a pre-heated 400°F (200°C) oven for 40 to 45 minutes, or until crispy.

ROASTED BUTTERNUT
2 lb (1 kg) peeled butternut squash, cut in chunks
2 tbsp (25 mL) extra-virgin olive oil
1 tsp (5 mL) kosher salt

POLENTA
4 cups (1 L) water
1 tbsp (15 mL) kosher salt
1 cup (250 mL) quick-cooking polenta
¼ cup (50 mL) extra-virgin olive oil or butter, divided
1 tbsp (15 mL) fresh thyme, or ½ tsp (2 mL) dried
½ tsp (2 mL) pepper

1. Place squash on a parchment-lined baking sheet. Toss with oil and salt. Roast in a preheated 375°F (190°C) oven for 45 minutes, or until tender. Puree. Measure out 3 cups (750 mL).
2. To prepare polenta, bring water to a boil in a large saucepan. Add salt. Stirring constantly, slowly add polenta. Cook, stirring, for 5 minutes, or until thick, creamy and coming away from sides of pan.
3. Stir squash, 2 tbsp (25 mL) oil, thyme and pepper into polenta. Taste and adjust seasonings if necessary.
4. Pour polenta into a 13- x 9-inch (3 L) oiled baking dish and chill until cold and firm.
5. Cut polenta into 3-inch (7.5 cm) squares. Place on a parchment-lined baking sheet and brush with remaining 2 tbsp (25 mL) oil. Bake in a preheated 400°F (200°C) oven for 20 to 30 minutes, or until browned.

MAKES 8 TO 10 SERVINGS

Grilled Endive

Belgian endive isn't just for salad. It is also delicious grilled and served as a side dish.

> 12 Belgian endives
> 2 tbsp (25 mL) extra-virgin olive oil
> 1 tbsp (15 mL) fresh thyme, or ½ tsp (2 mL) dried
> ½ tsp (2 mL) kosher salt
> Pinch pepper

1. Cut endives in half or quarters lengthwise (depending on their size), leaving them attached at stem end. Place in a large bowl.
2. Combine oil, thyme, salt and pepper and drizzle over endive. Toss gently.
3. Grill endive for 2 minutes per side.

MAKES 6 SERVINGS

Roasted Cherry Tomatoes with Basil

This is a delicious addition to almost any meal. It can be made ahead and served at room temperature. Serve it as a side dish or on top of chicken, fish or risotto as a sauce. Use it as a pizza or bruschetta topping or as a garnish for soups. It's also great tossed with pasta.

2 tbsp (25 mL) extra-virgin olive oil
4 cloves garlic, minced
1 tsp (5 mL) kosher salt
¼ tsp (1 mL) pepper
6 cups (1.5 L) cherry tomatoes
⅓ cup (75 mL) torn fresh basil leaves, divided

1. Combine oil, garlic, salt and pepper in a large bowl. Add tomatoes and about 1 tbsp (15 mL) basil. Mix well. Place on a baking sheet lined with parchment.
2. Roast in a preheated 400°F (200°C) oven for 30 to 45 minutes. Tomatoes should be soft but still hold their shape.
3. Toss with remaining ¼ cup (50 mL) basil.

MAKES 6 SERVINGS

Peaches Poached in Vanilla Syrup

I got this idea from John Higgins, who is in charge of the chef training programs at Toronto's George Brown College. He made it in spring with rhubarb, but you can adapt the recipe to any season by using plums, nectarines, pears or quince (peel the quince first and cook them for at least an hour, or until tender).

The peach syrup can also be used in drinks instead of plain sugar syrup—try using it instead of basil syrup in the martinis (page 18).

Serve this warm, cold or at room temperature.

6 peaches, ripe but firm
2 cups (500 mL) water
2 tbsp (25 mL) lemon juice
½ cup (125 mL) honey
1 vanilla bean, or 1 tsp (5 mL) vanilla paste
6 scoops vanilla ice cream or non-dairy frozen dessert, optional
1½ cups (375 mL) crumbled biscotti

1. Cut peaches in half and remove pits. (Do not bother to peel, as skins will slip off easily later.)
2. In a shallow saucepan, combine peaches, water, lemon juice and honey. Split vanilla bean and scrape out seeds. Add seeds and bean to saucepan (or add vanilla paste). Water should just cover peaches. Bring to a boil. Reduce heat and simmer gently for 10 to 15 minutes, or until peaches are tender. Remove peaches from syrup and slip off skins.
3. Place syrup over medium-high heat and cook for about 5 to 10 minutes, watching carefully, until reduced to about 1½ cups (375 mL).
4. To serve, place one or two peach halves in each serving bowl (I like to use stemless martini glasses). Add a scoop of ice cream, if using. Sprinkle with crumbled biscotti.

MAKES 6 SERVINGS

Gwen's Almond Biscotti

My good friend Gwen Berkowitz is the best cook. I could eat her food forever. When she gives me a recipe I know it will work and I know it will taste delicious. These biscotti are a great example. She has been making them for years, and remembers finding the recipe in the *Kinnereth Cookbook*. Special K is the secret ingredient.

I always bake biscotti on two cookie sheets (stacked) to help keep the cookies from burning.

   3 eggs
   1 cup (250 mL) granulated sugar
   1 cup (250 mL) vegetable oil
   1 tsp (5 mL) vanilla paste or pure vanilla extract
   2 cups (500 mL) all-purpose flour
   ½ tsp (2 mL) kosher salt
   2 tsp (10 mL) baking powder
   2 cups (500 mL) Special K cereal
   1 ½ cups (375 mL) coarsely chopped almonds

1. In a large bowl, beat eggs and sugar until light. Beat in oil and vanilla.
2. In a separate bowl, combine flour, salt and baking powder. Stir flour mixture into eggs. Stir in cereal and almonds. Mixture will be sticky. Refrigerate for a few hours or freeze for 30 minutes.
3. Shape mixture into eight logs about 6 inches (15 cm) long and 2 inches (5 cm) wide. Arrange about 2 inches (5 cm) apart on double stacked baking sheets lined with parchment paper.
4. Bake in a preheated 350°F (180°C) oven for 20 to 25 minutes, or until puffed and golden. Remove from oven and reduce oven temperature to 325°F (160°C). Cool biscotti for 10 minutes. With a serrated knife, cut logs into slices ¾ inch (2 cm) thick and arrange standing up or flat on baking sheets. Return to oven and bake for 15 to 20 minutes, or until lightly browned. (Turn after 10 minutes if you are baking them flat.)

MAKES ABOUT 60 COOKIES

thanksgiving

SERVES 8

We used to share a cottage with my sister, Jane, and her family, and we always celebrated Thanksgiving there. The kids would gather leaves to decorate the table, and we would cook a turkey in the ancient oven that came with the cottage. It must have been at least forty years old. The oven was calibrated incorrectly—we always had to guess whether something was ready (if it hadn't already burned)—which meant a large turkey could be ready hours too early, or too late. It's too bad I didn't know about laid-back turkey then. It cooks in less than an hour and a half and makes carving a breeze, and maybe we would have been more laid-back, too.

Many people don't realize how much easier Thanksgiving dinner can be if you make things ahead. The sangria, carrot spread, soup, stuffing, sweet potatoes, cranberry sauce, gravy and tart can all be made in advance, but a roast never tastes as good when it's reheated.

Ginger Pear Sangria

To make a non-alcoholic version of this, use ginger ale or sparkling juice instead of sparkling wine, and omit the pear liqueur.

> 1 1-inch (2.5 cm) piece fresh ginger, peeled and grated
> 3 cups (750 mL) pear nectar
> ¼ cup (50 mL) sugar syrup (page 86)
> ¼ cup (50 mL) pear liqueur or vodka, optional, divided
> 1 pear, cored and diced
> 1 tbsp (15 mL) lemon juice
> 2 tbsp (25 mL) finely chopped candied ginger
> Ice cubes
> 3 cups (750 mL) sparkling white wine or dry white wine

1. In a pitcher, combine ginger and pear nectar. Stir in sugar syrup and 2 tbsp (25 mL) pear liqueur, if using. Refrigerate.
2. In a small bowl, soak pear in remaining 2 tbsp (25 mL) liqueur and lemon juice. Refrigerate.
3. Place a little diced pear and candied ginger in each wine glass and add ice cubes. Pour in ⅓ cup (75 mL) pear ginger juice and ⅓ cup (75 mL) sparkling wine for each drink.

MAKES 8 SERVINGS

Roasted Carrot and Butternut Spread with Pita

This is a great appetizer, or you can put it on the table instead of butter or olive oil. You can also sprinkle the top with ½ cup (125 mL) diced feta cheese. Serve it with plain or grilled pita with za'atar (page 7).

> 1 lb (500 g) carrots, cut in chunks
> 1 lb (500 g) peeled butternut or buttercup squash or pumpkin, cut in chunks
> ¼ cup (50 mL) extra-virgin olive oil, divided
> 1 tsp (5 mL) chopped fresh rosemary, or ¼ tsp (1 mL) dried
> 1 tsp (5 mL) fresh thyme, or ¼ tsp (1 mL) dried
> 1 tsp (5 mL) kosher salt
> ¼ tsp (1 mL) pepper
> 1 head garlic
> 1 tbsp (15 mL) honey
> ½ tsp (2 mL) ground cumin
> 1 tbsp (15 mL) lemon juice
> 1 tsp (5 mL) pureed chipotles or chipotle Tabasco
> ½ cup (125 mL) pitted black olives, cut up if large
> 1 tbsp (15 mL) chopped fresh cilantro

1. Toss carrots and squash with 2 tbsp (25 mL) oil, rosemary, thyme, salt and pepper. Spread on a parchment-lined baking sheet. Cut top quarter off garlic head and brush with a little of the remaining 2 tbsp (25 mL) olive oil and a little of the honey. Wrap in foil and place on baking sheet. Drizzle remaining honey over vegetables.
2. Roast vegetables and garlic in a preheated 375°F (190°C) oven for 45 minutes, or until tender. Cool.
3. Place vegetables in a food processor. Squeeze in roasted garlic pulp. Add remaining oil, cumin, lemon juice and chipotles. Puree. Taste and adjust seasonings.
4. Spread mixture on a serving platter and top with olives and cilantro.

MAKES ABOUT 2 CUPS (500 ML)

Sweet Chili Tomato Soup with Cherry Tomatoes

I have never really liked tomato soup, but this one is so spectacular that even I can't resist it. It is sweet and spicy, smooth and chunky all at the same time.

Instead of serving this in soup bowls for the first course, I often serve it as an extra appetizer in shooter glasses—omit the cherry tomatoes and drizzle each serving with a little coconut milk if you wish.

2 tbsp (25 mL) extra-virgin olive oil
1 onion, chopped
2 cloves garlic, finely chopped
1 tbsp (15 mL) chopped fresh ginger
1 tsp (5 mL) ground cumin
½ tsp (2 mL) ground cinnamon
1 28-oz (796 mL) can plum tomatoes, with juices
2 cups (500 mL) chicken stock, vegetable stock or water
2 tbsp (25 mL) honey
2 tbsp (25 mL) lemon juice
2 tbsp (25 mL) sweet Thai chili sauce
Salt to taste

GARNISH
2 tbsp (25 mL) extra-virgin olive oil
2 cloves garlic, finely chopped
4 cups (1 L) cherry or grape tomatoes
Salt and pepper to taste

1. Heat oil in a large saucepan. Add onion, garlic and ginger. Cook gently for 5 minutes. Add cumin and cinnamon. Cook for 1 minute.
2. Add canned tomatoes, breaking up tomatoes with a wooden spoon. Add stock and bring to a boil. Reduce heat and simmer gently for 20 minutes.
3. Puree soup and return to heat. Add honey, lemon juice, sweet chili sauce and salt. Cook for 5 minutes.
4. Meanwhile, to prepare garnish, heat 2 tbsp (25 mL) oil in a large skillet over medium-high heat. Add garlic and cook for 1 minute. Add cherry tomatoes and cook for 5 to 10 minutes, or just until they split open. Season with salt and pepper.
5. Serve soup in shallow bowls with some cherry tomatoes.

MAKES 8 SERVINGS

Laid-back Roast Turkey with Cornbread Stuffing

This turkey is like no other. It is a take-off on an old Julia Child recipe that will stay young forever. It is moist and juicy and cooks in half the time as a regular turkey. When I "cooked" this on CBC's *Sounds Like Canada* with Shelagh Rogers and food historian Liz Driver, it caused a big reaction. Liz said a turkey had to be served whole as it is the meal's centerpiece. Shelagh said it tasted great but looked as though it had been run over by a truck!

I actually think my laid-back turkey looks gorgeous. And everyone agrees it is the best they have ever tasted. (You can use this stuffing in a traditional turkey as well. Use home-made cornbread, buy cornbread or cornbread muffins, or just use more regular bread.)

First things first. Be sure to buy a good turkey. A fresh organic or naturally raised turkey is my choice. A turkey weighing around 15 pounds (7 kg) is best for this recipe. Ask the butcher to butterfly it for you, leaving the drumsticks and wing bones in but removing the breast and thigh bones (keep the bones so you can use them for stock).

To make sure the turkey is not overcooked, use a meat thermometer. Because the stuffing is under the turkey and not inside it, the turkey meat will be safe to eat once it reaches 165°F (75°C). (A conventional stuffed turkey will be 180°F/82°C by the time the stuffing reaches 165°F.) Carving the laid-back turkey is also easy, and guests who love the wings or drumsticks can still have them.

So take a chance and break tradition—it is worth it.

1 15-lb (7 kg) fresh organic or free-range turkey, butterflied and partially boned out

3 tbsp (45 mL) extra-virgin olive oil

1 tbsp (15 mL) paprika

1 tbsp (15 mL) kosher salt

CORNBREAD STUFFING

2 tbsp (25 mL) extra-virgin olive oil

2 onions, chopped

4 cloves garlic, finely chopped

2 stalks celery, chopped

1 sweet red pepper or poblano pepper, peeled, seeded and diced

1 jalapeño, seeded and finely chopped, optional

¼ cup (50 mL) chopped fresh sage

¼ cup (50 mL) chopped fresh parsley

1 tbsp (15 mL) fresh thyme

8 cups (2 L) diced cornbread (page 00)

2 cups (500 mL) diced crusty bread

1 cup (250 mL) chicken stock or turkey stock, approx.

Salt and pepper to taste

1. Place turkey flat on a large parchment-lined baking sheet. Combine oil, paprika and salt and rub over both sides of turkey. Roast skin side down in a preheated 425°F (220°C) oven for 15 minutes to partially cook underside.

2. Meanwhile, to prepare stuffing, in a large, deep skillet or Dutch oven, heat oil over medium-high heat. Add onions and garlic. Cook for 3 minutes. Add celery, red pepper and jalapeño and cook for 10 minutes, or until tender. Add sage, parsley, thyme, cornbread and bread and combine well. Drizzle with stock and combine. Season with salt and pepper.

3. Spread cornbread mixture in a large parchment-lined roasting pan. Place turkey flat, skin side up, on top of stuffing (use heavy rubber gloves to transfer turkey).

4. Reduce oven temperature to 350°F (180°C). Roast turkey for 1¼ to 1½ hours, or until a meat thermometer registers 165°F (75°C) when inserted into thickest part of breast or thigh.

5. Slice turkey across breast and serve with stuffing.

MAKES 8 TO 10 SERVINGS

Cremini Mushroom Gravy

Cremini is just a sexy name for brown button mushrooms. They are actually immature portobellos, and I always use them instead of portobellos if the mushrooms are going to be finely chopped or pureed or strained out of a sauce. They are a little more gentle tasting than the large portobellos but delicious nonetheless, and they are less expensive.

> 3 tbsp (45 mL) extra-virgin olive oil or cooked turkey drippings
> ½ lb (250 g) cremini (brown button) mushrooms, sliced
> ¼ cup (50 mL) all-purpose flour
> 3 cups (750 mL) turkey stock or chicken stock
> 2 tbsp (25 mL) soy sauce
> 2 tbsp (25 mL) Port or brandy
> 2 tbsp (25 mL) lemon juice
> 1 tbsp (15 mL) Worcestershire sauce
> ½ tsp (2 mL) hot red pepper sauce
> Salt and pepper to taste

1. Heat oil in a large saucepan over medium heat. Add mushrooms and cook gently for 5 to 10 minutes, or until any liquid has evaporated. Sprinkle with flour and cook for 3 minutes.
2. Add stock and, whisking, bring to a boil. Add soy sauce, Port, lemon juice, Worcestershire and hot pepper sauce.
3. Reduce heat and cook gently for 10 minutes (you don't want this to be too thick). Add salt and pepper.
4. Strain sauce into a clean saucepan and reheat.

MAKES ABOUT 3 CUPS (750 ML)

Turkey or Chicken Stock

In a large saucepan, combine about 3 lb (1.5 kg) raw turkey or chicken bones, 1 chopped onion, 1 chopped carrot and 1 chopped stalk celery. Add water to cover by a couple of inches, bring to a boil and skim off any scum. Reduce heat, cover and simmer, uncovered, for 1½ to 2 hours. Strain.

Spiced Cranberry Port Sauce

It is so easy to make cranberry sauce that once you cook your own you'll never serve store-bought again. It is great just made traditionally with water and sugar, but Jennifer Mahoney, who works with me at the cooking school, adds orange, Port and spices—an idea she got when she worked at the Four Seasons.

If you do not have Port, just use more orange juice. This is also great used as a spread on turkey sandwiches.

½ cup (125 mL) Port
½ cup (125 mL) orange juice
1 cinnamon stick, broken
4 whole cloves
2 star anise
3 cups (750 mL) fresh or frozen cranberries
1 cup (250 mL) brown sugar
1 tbsp (15 mL) grated orange peel

1. In a large saucepan, combine Port, orange juice, cinnamon, cloves and star anise. Bring to a boil. Reduce heat and simmer gently, covered, for 5 to 10 minutes to infuse flavors of spices. Remove spices from pan.
2. Add cranberries, sugar and orange peel and simmer for 5 to 10 minutes, or until cranberries pop and sauce thickens. (It will thicken more when cold.)
3. Pour sauce into a bowl and chill. Serve cold.

MAKES 2 CUPS (500 ML)

Sweet Potato Mash with Vanilla and Chipotles

Sweet potatoes are perfect for a special dinner as they are so bright, colorful—and sweet. They do not have nearly as much starch as regular potatoes so they don't need much liquid when mashed. They also make a great topping for shepherd's pie (page 89). Sometimes people (kids) don't think they like sweet potatoes, but if you can get them to taste this, they will change their minds.

> 3 lb (1.5 kg) sweet potatoes, peeled and cut in chunks
> ¼ cup (50 mL) extra-virgin olive oil or butter
> 2 tbsp (25 mL) orange juice
> 1 tsp (5 mL) vanilla paste or pure vanilla extract
> 1 tsp (5 mL) kosher salt
> 1 tsp (5 mL) pureed chipotles or chipotle Tabasco, optional

1. Place sweet potatoes in a large pot of salted water. Bring to a boil and cook for about 20 minutes, or until tender. Drain well and mash coarsely. (Alternatively, sweet potatoes can be pricked with a fork and baked, unpeeled, on a baking sheet in a preheated 400°F/200°C oven for 45 to 60 minutes, or until very tender. Cool slightly, halve and then scrape cooked flesh out of skins.)

2. Add oil, orange juice, vanilla, salt and chipotles, if using. Mash until smooth. Taste and adjust seasonings if necessary.

3. Serve immediately or swirl or pipe into a greased baking dish and bake, covered, in a preheated 350°F (180°C) oven for 20 minutes, or until very hot.

MAKES 8 SERVINGS

Coconut Sweet Potato Mash

Add ½ cup (125 mL) coconut milk instead of olive oil and orange juice. Vanilla and chipotles are optional.

Maple Sweet Potato Mash

Add 2 tbsp (25 mL) maple syrup. Omit oil, vanilla and chipotles.

Sautéed Snow Peas with Garlic

This simple recipe brightens any plate and is so easy to make. You blanch the snow peas ahead and just reheat them in olive oil with garlic before serving.

   You can also make this using green beans or Brussels sprouts. Blanch them for 5 minutes and then sauté the beans for 1 to 2 minutes; cut sprouts in half and sauté for 5 minutes.

   1½ lb (750 g) snow peas, trimmed and cut in half on diagonal
   2 tbsp (25 mL) extra-virgin olive oil
   2 cloves garlic, finely chopped
   1 tsp (5 mL) kosher salt

1. Bring a large pot of water to a boil. Add snow peas and cook for 30 seconds. Drain, rinse with cold water and pat dry.
2. Just before serving, heat oil in a large skillet over medium heat. Add garlic. Cook gently for 1 to 2 minutes, but do not brown.
3. Add snow peas and cook for 1 to 2 minutes, or until heated through and tender. Season with salt.

MAKES 8 SERVINGS

Green Salad with Walnut Dressing

This dressing comes from Toronto chef Anthony Rose. He drizzles it on grilled radicchio, and sprinkles the salad with crumbled goat cheese.

- ¾ cup (175 mL) coarsely chopped toasted walnuts, divided
- ½ cup (125 mL) extra-virgin olive oil
- 2 tbsp (25 mL) Champagne vinegar or good white wine vinegar
- 1 tbsp (15 mL) lemon juice
- ¾ tsp (4 mL) kosher salt
- ¼ tsp (1 mL) pepper
- 12 cups (3 L) mixed baby greens
- 2 tbsp (25 mL) fresh oregano

1. To prepare dressing, in a blender or food processor, blend ½ cup (125 mL) walnuts with oil and vinegar until smooth. Blend in lemon juice, salt and pepper.
2. Place greens in a large bowl and toss with as much dressing as you need (refrigerate or freeze the rest). Sprinkle with remaining walnuts and oregano.

MAKES 8 SERVINGS

Rustic Apple Tart

Nothing beats apple pie. This is a wonderful homey version that is great for beginners because you don't have to worry about rolling the pastry into any particular shape. I like to use Spy or Golden Delicious apples.

Serve this with caramel sauce (page 56) and a scoop of vanilla ice cream or non-dairy frozen dessert if you wish, or simply dust with sifted icing sugar.

ALL-PURPOSE PASTRY
2 cups (500 mL) all-purpose flour
Pinch kosher salt
Pinch granulated sugar
1 cup (250 mL) butter or margarine, cold, cut in bits
⅓ cup (75 mL) ice water, approx.

FILLING

6 apples (about 2 to 2½ lb/1 to 1.25 kg), peeled, cored and thickly sliced

½ cup (125 mL) brown sugar

¼ cup (50 mL) all-purpose flour

1 tsp (5 mL) ground cinnamon

1 egg, lightly beaten

2 tbsp (25 mL) coarse sugar

1. To prepare pastry, in a large bowl, combine flour, salt and granulated sugar. Add butter and rub into flour using your fingertips or a pastry blender. Butter should be in tiny pieces but still visible. Sprinkle with ice water and gather into a rough ball. Add more water if necessary. Form dough into a flat disk, wrap in plastic wrap and refrigerate for 30 minutes.

2. To prepare filling, in a large bowl, combine apples, brown sugar, flour and cinnamon.

3. On a lightly floured work surface, roll dough into a 16-inch (40 cm) circle (or whatever shape you end up with!). Transfer pastry to a parchment-lined baking sheet.

4. Spread apples in a 9-inch (23 cm) circle in middle of pastry. Bring pastry up over apples, leaving hole in center.

5. Brush pastry with beaten egg and sprinkle with coarse sugar. Bake in a preheated 425°F (220°C) oven for 20 minutes. Reduce heat to 375°F (190°C) and continue to bake for 40 to 50 minutes, or until crust is golden and apples are very tender.

MAKES 8 SERVINGS

Caramel Sauce

In a large saucepan, stir 1 cup (250 mL) granulated sugar and ¼ cup (50 mL) water over medium-high heat until sugar comes to a boil. Brush any sugar down sides of pan with a pastry brush dipped in cold water. Cook, without stirring, for 6 to 8 minutes, or until caramel turns deep golden. Remove from heat and carefully add ¾ cup (175 mL) whipping cream. Heat gently until smooth. Cool.

Makes about 1 cup (250 mL).

SPARKLING POMEGRANATE SANGRIA

EGG AND SMOKED TROUT SALAD WITH CAPERS

YEMENITE CHICKEN SOUP

RIB ROAST WITH GARLIC MUSTARD RUB

COUNTRY MASH

ROASTED RATATOUILLE

SPINACH AND ORANGE SALAD WITH HONEY ORANGE DRESSING

RUTHIE'S APPLE CAKE

CHOCOLATE BARK WITH ALMONDS, GINGER AND ORANGE PEEL

GINGER CRACKLE COOKIES

rosh hashanah

SERVES 8 TO 10

The Jewish new year falls in September or October, and I always think it feels like the right time to celebrate a new year. Summer is over, the kids go back to school, and we feel all the excitement (and anxiety) of a new cycle beginning.

Rosh Hashanah is a holiday with many food themes. We cook foods that are traditional to our family, we eat seasonal fruits (such as pomegranates) for the first time that year, we celebrate the harvest by eating lots of vegetables, and we eat foods that are sweet (such as apples and challah dipped in honey) to wish everyone a sweet new year.

Everything can be prepared ahead except for roasting the meat and ratatouille and tossing the salad (or the ratatouille can be made ahead and served at room temperature).

44

Sparkling Pomegranate Sangria

It used to be almost impossible to find pomegranate juice, but now that it has been found to be high in antioxidants, it is almost as common as orange juice. It tastes delicious in cocktails—use it instead of cranberry juice in cosmopolitans to make pomtinis (page 62).

You can sometimes buy the pomegranate seeds themselves, but it is much more fun to open a real pomegranate. It is said that each pomegranate contains 613 seeds (the number of commandments in the Torah), but if you do count them you may find yourself a few hundred short!

You can use regular instead of sparkling Shiraz. For a non-alcoholic version of this, use soda water instead of sparkling wine and frozen orange juice concentrate instead of orange liqueur.

½ cup (125 mL) orange liqueur
¼ cup (50 mL) granulated sugar
3 cups (750 mL) pomegranate juice
1 orange, cut in wedges and sliced
½ cup (125 mL) pomegranate seeds, optional
3 cups (750 mL) sparkling Shiraz or sparkling dry white wine
2 cups (500 mL) ice cubes

1. In a large pitcher, combine orange liqueur and sugar. Stir until sugar dissolves.
2. Add pomegranate juice, orange slices and pomegranate seeds, if using. Stir well. Cover and refrigerate until ready to serve.
3. Stir in sparkling wine just before serving. Add ice cubes to glasses and pour sangria over top.

MAKES 8 SERVINGS

Cutting a Pomegranate

Cut a thin incision around the circumference. Immerse the pomegranate in a large bowl of water and gently pull the skin apart where you have cut. (My mother never did this, and if you don't, either, be sure to wear red or black, because it can be messy.) The seeds will sink and the pith will rise to the top. Discard the pith, drain and use the seeds in drinks and salads (you can also freeze them).

Egg and Smoked Trout Salad with Capers

Serve this delicious version of egg salad with grilled challah (page 94), rye or black bread. Brush one side of the bread lightly with extra-virgin olive oil, sprinkle with kosher salt and grill on both sides.

You can also use this salad in sandwiches or gougères (page 258).

Be sure to remove all the tiny bones from the smoked fish.

6 hard-cooked eggs, peeled
8 oz (250 g) smoked trout or whitefish fillets, boned and flaked
¼ cup (50 mL) diced sweet pickle
1 tbsp (15 mL) capers, rinsed and drained
¼ cup (50 mL) mayonnaise
1 tbsp (15 mL) lemon juice (or to taste)
1 shallot, finely chopped
1 tbsp (15 mL) chopped fresh tarragon
1 tsp (5 mL) Dijon mustard
Salt and pepper to taste
2 tbsp (25 mL) chopped fresh chives

1. Chop eggs and combine with trout, pickle and capers in a bowl.
2. In a separate small bowl, combine mayonnaise, lemon juice, shallot, tarragon and mustard.
3. Add mayonnaise to egg and trout mixture and combine. Season to taste with salt and pepper and sprinkle with chives.

MAKES 2½ CUPS (625 ML)

Hard-cooked Eggs

This method, adapted from Jacques Pépin, is the best way I've found to hard-cook eggs so that they peel easily, do not have a green ring around the yolk and are not overooked. Bring enough water to a boil to cover eggs by a few inches. Add 1 tbsp (15 mL) salt. Place eggs gently in boiling water. When water returns to a boil, cover and turn off heat. Let eggs sit in water for 14 minutes.

Drain eggs and cover with cold water. Crack eggs gently against sides of pot and let eggs rest in cold water for 15 minutes. Peel.

Yemenite Chicken Soup

My friend Hanoch Drori introduces me to all kinds of Israeli recipes. Since he moved to Canada ten years ago, he has become part of our family. His mother makes a wonderful Yemenite chicken soup with hawayij (an Arab blend of spices), hilbeh (fenugreek whipped with water) and z'houg (cilantro pesto). I make my own simpler version. I even add Ashkenazi matzah balls, combining two chicken soup traditions.

I always like to make chicken soup a day ahead so I can strain the soup, refrigerate it overnight and then remove all the solidified fat that rises to the surface. Save the meat and vegetables separately to serve in the soup. (If you are serving the soup on the same day, spoon off the fat or use a gravy separator.)

1 4-lb (2 kg) chicken, cut up

12 cups (3 L) cold water

2 onions, peeled and cut in half

4 carrots, cut in half

2 stalks celery with leaves, cut in half

1 leek, well washed and cut in large pieces

1 tbsp (15 mL) tomato paste

1 tbsp (15 mL) cumin seeds

1 tbsp (15 mL) black peppercorns

1 tbsp (15 mL) caraway seeds

1 tbsp (15 mL) coriander seeds

2 tsp (10 mL) kosher salt

1 tsp (5 mL) cardamom seeds

½ tsp (2 mL) saffron threads

CILANTRO PESTO (Z'HOUG)

2 cloves garlic, peeled

1 jalapeño, seeded and coarsely chopped (or to taste)

1 cup (250 mL) packed fresh cilantro

½ tsp (2 mL) kosher salt

⅓ cup (75 mL) extra-virgin olive oil

1. Place chicken in a large saucepan or Dutch oven. Add cold water to cover chicken. Bring to a boil (this will take 10 to 15 minutes). Remove and discard scum that rises to surface.
2. Add onions, carrots, celery, leek, tomato paste, cumin, peppercorns, caraway, coriander, salt, cardamom and saffron. Simmer, uncovered, for 2 hours.
3. Strain soup and cut carrots, celery and onions into bite-sized pieces. Remove chicken from bones and reserve with vegetables. Refrigerate soup and chicken separately. Juices may turn into jelly but don't worry—it's a good thing. Discard solidified fat from top of soup.
4. To prepare z'houg, in a food processor, blend garlic, jalapeño, cilantro, salt and oil until mixture forms a paste.
5. Before serving, reheat soup with chicken and vegetables. Serve with a spoonful of z'houg.

MAKES 8 TO 10 SERVINGS

Matzah Balls

In a bowl, combine 4 eggs, 1 cup (250 mL) matzah meal, 1 tbsp (15 mL) kosher salt, ¼ cup (50 mL) chicken soup or water and 3 tbsp (45 mL) vegetable oil or chicken fat. Mix just until combined. Cover and refrigerate for 30 minutes.

Bring a large pot of water to a boil.

With wet hands, very gently shape mixture into about 20 balls. Do not worry if they are not all the same shape or size. Do not overhandle.

Gently drop matzah balls into boiling water. When water returns to a boil, reduce heat, cover and simmer gently for 30 to 35 minutes, or until matzah balls have doubled in size and risen to surface.

Spoon matzah balls into hot soup, or spoon into bowls and pour hot soup over top.

Makes about 20 matzah balls.

Rib Roast with Garlic Mustard Rub

When my mother wanted to cook a really special dinner, she made a standing rib roast, and to this day I still think it's special.

   If you are using a standing rib roast, be sure to tell the butcher to cut off the chine bone to make it easy to carve between the ribs. If this means the roast won't stand up in the roasting pan, just wedge a couple of peeled onions underneath.

   Use a meat thermometer to make sure the roast is cooked to medium-rare. (Don't take a chance after paying so much for such a gorgeous roast.)

¼ cup (50 mL) Dijon mustard
2 tbsp (25 mL) extra-virgin olive oil
4 cloves garlic, minced
1 tbsp (15 mL) finely chopped fresh rosemary, or 1 tsp (5 mL) dried
1 tbsp (15 mL) fresh thyme, or 1 tsp (5 mL) dried
1 tbsp (15 mL) kosher salt
1 tbsp (15 mL) pepper
1 6-lb (3 kg) standing rib roast, boneless rib roast or strip sirloin roast
2 shallots, thinly sliced
¾ cup (175 mL) dry red wine
1 cup (250 mL) beef stock

1. In a small bowl, combine mustard, oil, garlic, rosemary, thyme, salt and pepper.
2. Smear roast all over with mustard rub. Place in a shallow roasting pan, fat side up.
3. Roast meat in a preheated 425°F (220°C) oven for 20 minutes. Reduce heat to 375°F (190°C) and continue to roast for 1¼ to 2 hours, or until a meat thermometer reaches 130°F (55°C) for medium-rare. Transfer roast to a cutting board and allow to rest for 20 minutes before carving.
4. While roast is resting, place roasting pan on stove over medium-high heat and skim off fat. Add shallots and wine and cook until reduced to 2 tbsp (25 mL). Add stock and cook until reduced to ½ cup (125 mL).
5. To carve, remove string from roast. Cut off bones in one piece by cutting between meat and bones. Cut bones apart and serve with meat (to guests who want them the most!). Turn roast over on carving board so it is sitting boned side down and carve into slices. Spoon juices over roast when serving.

MAKES 10 SERVINGS

Individual Yorkshire Puddings

Yorkshire pudding is a traditional accompaniment for roast beef, and many people can't do without it.

Place muffin pan in oven and preheat oven to 350°F (180°C).

Meanwhile, combine 1½ cups (375 mL) all-purpose flour and 1 tsp (5 mL) kosher salt in a large bowl.

In a separate bowl, whisk 1½ cups (375 mL) warm milk (or soy milk) with 3 eggs. Whisk into flour mixture. Do not overmix or worry about little lumps.

Brush hot muffin pan with roast drippings. Spoon about ¼ cup (50 mL) batter into each cup. Bake for 30 to 35 minutes, or until puffed and browned. Serve hot. (You can also bake the batter in mini muffin pans. Use 2 tbsp / 25 mL batter per cup and bake for 25 minutes.)

Makes 12 puddings.

Country Mash

This is a delicious blend of root vegetables that goes well with any roast or braised dish. Even people who don't think they would ever eat a parsnip seem to love it. It also makes a great topping for shepherd's pie (page 89).

If you make the mash ahead, transfer it to a 13- x 9-inch (3 L) baking dish and reheat, covered, at 350°F (180°C) for 30 to 40 minutes.

2 lb (1 kg) sweet potatoes, peeled and cut in chunks
2 lb (1 kg) Yukon gold potatoes, peeled and cut in chunks
1 lb (500 g) parsnips, peeled and cut in chunks
1 lb (500 g) carrots, squash, turnip, celery root or parsley root, peeled and cut in chunks
½ cup (125 mL) extra-virgin olive oil or butter
½ cup (125 mL) chicken stock or cream, hot, approx.
2 tsp (10 mL) kosher salt
1 small bunch chives, optional

1. In a large pot, cover sweet potatoes, regular potatoes, parsnips and carrots with plenty of salted water. Bring to a boil and cook for 25 to 30 minutes, or until tender. Drain well.
2. Add oil, stock and salt. Mash coarsely. (I like to leave it a bit chunky.) Taste and adjust seasonings if necessary. Spoon into a serving dish.
3. If using chives, cut into 2-inch (5 cm) pieces and sprinkle over vegetables.

MAKES 8 TO 10 SERVINGS

Roasted Ratatouille

Ratatouille—a French Provençal vegetable stew made with onions, garlic, zucchini, eggplant and tomatoes—has always been delicious, but not that many people knew about it. Then the fabulously entertaining animated film came out with the same name, and suddenly everyone knew about ratatouille.

This is a roasted version that I love. Roasting allows each veggie to maintain its integrity, without becoming mushy. Serve it as a side dish with meat or poultry, as a sauce with pasta, polenta or risotto, as a filling in omelets or quiches, or puree to make a soup.

I usually peel the peppers with a soft skin peeler, but a regular vegetable peeler works, too.

2 heads garlic
2 onions, peeled and cut in wedges
1 lb (500 g) Asian eggplants, cut in 1½-inch (4 cm) chunks
1 lb (500 g) zucchini, cut in 1½-inch (4 cm) chunks
¼ cup (50 mL) extra-virgin olive oil
1 tsp (5 mL) kosher salt
½ tsp (2 mL) pepper
3 tbsp (45 mL) fresh thyme, or 1 tsp (5 mL) dried
2 sweet red peppers, peeled, seeded and cut in wedges
2 sweet yellow peppers, peeled, seeded and cut in wedges
2 cups (500 mL) cherry tomatoes

1. Cut top quarter from heads of garlic. Wrap in foil in a single layer and place in a preheated 400°F (200°C) oven for 45 to 50 minutes, or until very soft and tender.
2. Meanwhile, place onions, eggplants and zucchini on a parchment-lined baking sheet. Drizzle with most of the oil, salt, pepper and thyme. Roast for 30 to 40 minutes, or until browned.
3. Place peppers and tomatoes on a separate parchment-lined baking sheet. Drizzle with remaining oil, salt, pepper and thyme. Roast for 20 minutes, or until tender and lightly browned. Tomatoes should be juicy.
4. Combine all roasted veggies in a large bowl. Squeeze roasted garlic into vegetables and toss gently. Serve hot or at room temperature.

MAKES 8 TO 10 SERVINGS

Spinach and Orange Salad with Honey Orange Dressing

This salad is refreshing and beautiful. Pomegranate molasses, which is made from reduced pomegranate juice, is available at Middle Eastern stores, specialty markets and gourmet shops.

> 2 tbsp (25 mL) pomegranate molasses
> 1 tbsp (15 mL) honey
> 3 tbsp (45 mL) orange juice
> ½ tsp (2 mL) kosher salt
> ¼ cup (50 mL) extra-virgin olive oil
> 1 lb (500 g) baby spinach (about 12 cups / 3 L)
> 2 large oranges, peeled and separated in segments
> 1 ripe avocado
> 1 cup (250 mL) pomegranate seeds (page 46), optional

1. In a small bowl, whisk together pomegranate molasses, honey, orange juice and salt. Whisk in oil.
2. Place spinach in a large bowl. Just before serving, toss spinach with dressing. Arrange oranges on top. Scoop out avocado on top of oranges and sprinkle with pomegranate seeds, if using.

MAKES 8 TO 10 SERVINGS

Ratatouille Tart

This is delicious served warm or cold for an appetizer, brunch, lunch or light supper. The baking time will depend on how deep your tart pan is.

Place 2 cups (500 mL) well-drained and chopped ratatouille in a partially baked (page 15) 9- or 10-inch (23 or 25 cm) tart shell. Sprinkle with 1 cup (250 mL) grated Swiss cheese.

In a bowl, whisk together 3 eggs, 1 cup (250 mL) cream or milk and salt and pepper to taste. Pour over vegetables.

Bake in a preheated 375°F (190°C) oven for 30 to 40 minutes, or until custard is just set in center.

Let tart rest for 10 minutes before serving.

Makes 8 servings.

Ruthie's Apple Cake

Almost everyone's mom has a favorite apple cake. This is my mother's. It is delicious served plain or with caramel sauce (page 43).

2 eggs
1 cup (250 mL) granulated sugar
⅔ cup (150 mL) vegetable oil
¼ cup (50 mL) orange juice
2 tsp (10 mL) vanilla paste or pure vanilla extract
1½ cups (375 mL) all-purpose flour
2 tsp (10 mL) baking powder
¼ tsp (1 mL) kosher salt
½ cup (125 mL) brown sugar
1 tsp (5 mL) ground cinnamon
2 lb (1 kg) McIntosh apples (4 or 5), peeled, cored and coarsely chopped
½ cup (125 mL) chopped toasted walnuts, optional
2 tbsp (25 mL) coarse sugar

1. With an electric mixer, beat eggs and granulated sugar in a bowl until very light. Beat in oil. Beat in orange juice and vanilla.
2. In a separate bowl, combine flour, baking powder and salt. Add to egg mixture and stir just until combined.
3. In a third bowl, combine brown sugar, cinnamon, apples and nuts, if using.
4. Spread about half the batter in an oiled and parchment-lined 9-inch (23 cm) spring-form pan. Spoon apples on top. Drizzle remaining batter on top of apples. Do not worry if batter doesn't cover apples completely. Sprinkle with coarse sugar.
5. Bake in a preheated 350°F (180°C) oven for 50 to 60 minutes, or until a cake tester comes out clean. If cake is browning too much, cover loosely with foil and reduce oven temperature to 325°F (160°C).

MAKES 8 TO 12 SERVINGS

Chocolate Bark with Almonds, Ginger and Orange Peel

Nutritionist Fran Berkoff and I teach a course called "Ten Healthy Foods and How to Make Them Delicious." We usually serve this for dessert. Not only does it taste wonderful, but, in small quantities, it is a healthful treat. Researchers say 70 percent chocolate is a good source of antioxidants. With its fruit and nuts, this is also perfect for Rosh Hashanah, and it makes a great take-home gift. Use your favorite dried fruit and nuts.

12 oz (375 g) 70 percent dark chocolate, chopped
1½ cups (375 mL) coarsely chopped toasted almonds
½ cup (125 mL) chopped candied ginger
½ cup (125 mL) chopped candied orange peel
1½ tsp (7 mL) sea salt (e.g., Maldon)

1. Melt chocolate in a bowl set over simmering water or in a microwave for 1½ to 2 minutes. Remove from heat before chocolate is completely melted and stir to finish melting.
2. Stir in nuts, ginger and orange peel. Stir in salt.
3. Spread mixture ½ inch (1 cm) thick on a parchment-lined baking sheet and chill. Cut or break into chunks. Store in the freezer.

MAKES ABOUT 20 PIECES

Ginger Crackle Cookies

This is the perfect ginger cookie—robustly flavored with ginger and cinnamon. You can make giant cookies by doubling the amount of batter and baking for a few minutes longer.

⅔ cup (150 mL) vegetable oil
1 cup (250 mL) granulated sugar
1 egg
¼ cup (50 mL) molasses
2 cups (500 mL) all-purpose flour or whole wheat flour
2 tsp (10 mL) ground ginger
1 tsp (5 mL) ground cinnamon
1 tsp (5 mL) baking powder
1 tsp (5 mL) baking soda
¼ tsp (1 mL) kosher salt
½ cup (125 mL) coarse sugar

1. With an electric mixer or in a food processor, combine oil and granulated sugar. Beat in egg and molasses.
2. In a separate bowl, combine flour, ginger, cinnamon, baking powder, baking soda and salt. Stir into egg mixture. Refrigerate dough for 1 hour.
3. Shape dough into balls (1 tbsp/15 mL each). Roll in coarse sugar. Place on parchment-lined baking sheets with lots of room between cookies. Press down lightly.
4. Bake in a preheated 350°F (180°C) oven for 9 to 11 minutes, or until cookies are crackly but still chewy. Cool on racks.

MAKES 30 TO 36 COOKIES

POMTINIS

KEBABS ON CINNAMON STICKS

GRILLED EGGPLANT WITH TAHINA AND TOMATO LIME SALSA

CHICKEN TAGINE WITH HONEYED TOMATOES AND CHICKPEAS

OR

CHICKEN TAGINE WITH GREEN OLIVES AND PRESERVED LEMONS

COUSCOUS WITH PRESERVED LEMON, DATES AND ALMONDS

SALAD WITH POMEGRANATE DRESSING

INDIVIDUAL HALVAH SOUFFLÉS

israeli dinner

SERVES 8

I was raised in an Ashkenazi (Eastern European) Jewish household, so when I went to Israel for the first time, I was surprised to see a menu for Friday night dinner that featured carrot cumin soup followed by chicken with dried fruit and couscous instead of chicken soup with matzah balls followed by brisket and mashed potatoes. I really fell hard for those Middle Eastern Sephardic flavors, and now Rabbi Elyse Goldstein and I lead culinary tours to Israel to show people how delicious Israeli food can be.

I have given you two choices for the tagine—a sweeter tagine with tomatoes and chickpeas and a tarter one with olives and lemon. (A tagine refers to a traditional Moroccan cooking vessel as well as to the braised food that is cooked in it.)

Almost everything in this menu can be prepared ahead. Reheat the kebabs, tagine and couscous in a 350°F (180°C) oven. Assemble the soufflés ahead, refrigerate them, and put them in the oven just as you are finishing your main course.

Pomtinis

The first time I tasted fresh pomegranate juice in the market in Tel Aviv, I flipped. Freshly squeezed is amazing, but now that pomegranate juice is considered to be so healthful and full of antioxidants, you can buy commercial brands everywhere.

You can shake each martini, but if I am making more than a few of these I usually just make a big pitcher in advance and refrigerate it. Add ice just before serving or serve it straight up. Garnish with pomegranate seeds or rose petals. For those who aren't drinking, mix the pom juice with soda water, ginger ale or sparkling fruit juice.

1½ cups (375 mL) vodka
2½ cups (625 mL) pomegranate juice
¼ cup (50 mL) Pama (pomegranate liqueur) or orange liqueur

1. In a large pitcher, combine vodka, pomegranate juice and liqueur. Refrigerate until ready to serve.

MAKES 8 TO 10 SERVINGS

Kebabs on Cinnamon Sticks

These kebabs come from Ariel Porat, executive chef at the Dan Hotel in Herzliya. They are so cute and delicious. Make them with ground chicken or all beef or lamb if you prefer. You can also add a few tablespoons of whole or chopped pine nuts to the meat mixture. If the cinnamon sticks are too thick (double), cut or break them in half lengthwise.

Make these ahead and reheat them for 15 minutes in a preheated 350°F (180°C) oven. You can actually omit the step of browning the kebabs in a skillet, but the meat will not be as glazed. (If you omit the browning step, bake them at 400°F/200°C for 15 to 20 minutes.)

½ lb (250 g) ground beef
½ lb (250 g) ground lamb
2 tbsp (25 mL) finely chopped onion
1 clove garlic, minced
1 tsp (5 mL) ground cumin
¼ tsp (1 mL) ground cinnamon
2 tbsp (25 mL) chopped fresh cilantro
1 tsp (5 mL) finely chopped preserved lemon peel or grated lemon peel
1 tsp (5 mL) kosher salt
2 tbsp (25 mL) soda water
24 small (about 3 inches/7.5 cm) cinnamon sticks
1 tbsp (15 mL) extra-virgin olive oil

1. In a large bowl, combine beef, lamb, onion, garlic, cumin, ground cinnamon, cilantro, preserved lemon and salt. Knead together lightly. Add soda water and knead in.
2. Divide mixture into 24 balls. Shape each around the end of a cinnamon stick.
3. Heat oil in a heavy skillet over medium-high heat. Brown kebabs in batches for 1 to 2 minutes on each side.
4. Transfer kebabs to a parchment-lined baking sheet. Bake in a preheated 350°F (180°C) oven for 10 minutes.

MAKES 24 SMALL KEBABS

Grilled Eggplant with Tahina and Tomato Lime Salsa

In Israel, this dish is very popular and served in many different ways.

2 lb (1 kg) Asian eggplants (about 6)
2 tbsp (25 mL) extra-virgin olive oil
1 tsp (5 mL) kosher salt

TAHINA SAUCE
½ cup (125 mL) tahina
2 cloves garlic, minced
¼ cup (50 mL) lime juice or lemon juice
1 tsp (5 mL) kosher salt
Dash hot red pepper sauce
⅓ cup (75 mL) water, approx.

TOMATO LIME SALSA
1 tomato, seeded and chopped
1 clove garlic, minced
1 tbsp (15 mL) lime juice
1 tbsp (15 mL) extra-virgin olive oil
½ tsp (2 mL) kosher salt
2 tbsp (25 mL) chopped fresh cilantro
2 tbsp (25 mL) chopped fresh parsley

1. Trim eggplants and cut lengthwise into 3 or 4 long slices. Brush with oil and sprinkle with salt. Grill for 3 to 4 minutes per side, or until browned and cooked through. Arrange overlapping slices on a platter.
2. To prepare tahina sauce, in a bowl or food processor, combine tahina, garlic, lime juice, salt, hot pepper sauce and enough water to turn sauce white and thin it to a pourable consistency.
3. To prepare salsa, in a small bowl, combine tomato, garlic, lime juice, oil, salt, cilantro and parsley.
4. Drizzle tahina sauce over eggplant and sprinkle with salsa.

MAKES 6 SERVINGS

Chicken Tagine with Honeyed Tomatoes and Chickpeas

If I am serving buffet style, I like to make this with boneless chicken thighs, which stay moist and juicy and are easier to eat. (You can also use chicken breasts; just don't overcook them.) This can be made a day ahead and reheated, covered, at 350°F (180°C) for 30 minutes.

For the most flavorful cumin, buy cumin seeds. Toast the seeds in a dry skillet over medium heat until they turn slightly reddish and the aroma is fabulous. Cool. Grind in a spice grinder or in an old coffee grinder reserved for spices, and freeze.

Saffron, the most expensive spice in the world, is the dried stigmas of the crocus flower. Use it sparingly and buy threads so you know you're getting the real thing.

This recipe is also great made with lamb shanks. Cook them for 2 to 3 hours, or until very tender.

You can also serve this drizzled with tahina sauce (page 105) or charmoula (page 185).

1 tbsp (15 mL) kosher salt

1 tbsp (15 mL) paprika

1 tbsp (15 mL) ground cumin

4 lb (2 kg) boneless, skinless chicken thighs (about 16)

2 tbsp (25 mL) extra-virgin olive oil

2 onions, sliced

3 cloves garlic, finely chopped

1 tbsp (15 mL) chopped fresh ginger

2 tsp (10 mL) ground cumin

½ tsp (2 mL) ground cinnamon

½ tsp (2 mL) cayenne

¼ tsp (1 mL) saffron threads, crushed and dissolved in
   2 tbsp (25 mL) boiling water

1 28-oz (796 mL) can plum tomatoes, with juices, crushed

2 cups (500 mL) chicken stock

2 cups (500 mL) cooked or canned chickpeas

2 tbsp (25 mL) honey

1 tbsp (15 mL) lemon juice

Salt and pepper to taste

1 tbsp (15 mL) sesame seeds, toasted

¼ cup (50 mL) coarsely chopped fresh cilantro

1 lemon, thinly sliced, or peel of 1 preserved lemon, julienned

1. In a small bowl, combine salt, paprika and 1 tbsp (15 mL) cumin. Sprinkle mixture on chicken.

2. Heat oil in a large, deep skillet over medium-high heat. Add chicken in batches and cook for 5 to 8 minutes per side, or until browned. Transfer chicken to a large roasting pan.

3. Discard all but a few tablespoons of oil from skillet. Add onions, garlic and ginger. Reduce heat and cook gently for 10 minutes, scraping solidified juices from bottom of skillet. Add ½ cup (125 mL) water if necessary.

4. Add 2 tsp (10 mL) cumin, cinnamon and cayenne and cook for 30 seconds. Add saffron, tomatoes and stock. Bring to a boil. Reduce heat and cook gently for 20 minutes. Sauce should be as thick as a pasta sauce.

5. Add chickpeas and cook for 5 minutes. Stir in honey and lemon juice and season with salt and pepper.

6. Pour sauce over chicken. Bake in a preheated 350°F (180°C) oven for 20 to 25 minutes, or until chicken is cooked through.

7. Sprinkle chicken with sesame seeds and cilantro. Garnish with lemon slices.

MAKES 8 SERVINGS

Cooking Chickpeas

Soak 1 cup (250 mL) dried chickpeas in a large bowl of cold water in refrigerator overnight. Drain. Cook in a large pot of unsalted boiling water, covered, for 1 to 1½ hours, or until very tender. Drain well. You can make lots and freeze them.

Makes about 2 cups (500 mL).

Chicken Tagine with Green Olives and Preserved Lemons

This can be made ahead and reheated, covered, in a preheated 350°F (180°C) oven for 30 minutes (chicken thighs reheat the best). You can also use boneless, skinless chicken breasts or thighs.

1 tbsp (15 mL) paprika

1 tbsp (15 mL) kosher salt

1 tsp (5 mL) pepper

¼ tsp (1 mL) saffron threads

¼ tsp (1 mL) cayenne

8 chicken breasts or thighs (or a mixture), bone in, skin on
   (about 4 to 5 lb/2 to 2.5 kg total)

2 tbsp (25 mL) extra-virgin olive oil

3 large onions, sliced

3 cloves garlic, finely chopped

½ tsp (2 mL) hot red pepper flakes

2 cups (500 mL) pitted green olives (or half green and half black olives)

Peel of 1 preserved lemon, rinsed and thinly sliced,
   or 1 tbsp (15 mL) grated lemon peel

¼ cup (50 mL) chopped fresh parsley, divided

¼ cup (50 mL) chopped fresh cilantro, divided

1 lemon, thinly sliced

1. In a small bowl, combine paprika, salt, pepper, saffron and cayenne. Rub into chicken. Marinate for a few hours in refrigerator.
2. Heat oil in a large, deep skillet over medium-high heat. Cook chicken in batches for 5 to 8 minutes per side, or until browned. Transfer chicken to a large roasting pan.
3. Add onions to pan and cook for 10 to 15 minutes, or until browned. Add garlic and hot pepper flakes.
4. Spoon onions on top of chicken. Sprinkle with olives, preserved lemon and half the parsley and cilantro.
5. Bake in a preheated 350°F (180°C) oven for 25 to 30 minutes, or until chicken is cooked through and a meat thermometer reads 160°F (75°C). (Reduce heat to 350°F/180°C if chicken is browning too much.) Serve sprinkled with remaining parsley and cilantro and fresh lemon slices.

MAKES 8 SERVINGS

Preserved Lemons

You can buy preserved lemons in Middle Eastern stores, but it's easy to make them yourself.

Place ½ cup (125 mL) kosher salt in a 4-cup (1 L) preserving jar. Cut 3 or 4 lemons into quarters lengthwise, leaving stem ends attached. Fill lemons with kosher salt (about 1½ cups / 375 mL) and pack in jar tightly, open ends up. Cover lemons with 1½ cups (375 mL) freshly squeezed lemon juice (about 6 lemons), add lid and refrigerate for 4 weeks.

Rinse the preserved lemons before using. Use just the peel and discard the pulp (and pith if it is very thick). The chopped peel of 1 preserved lemon should yield about ¼ cup (50 mL).

Couscous with Preserved Lemon, Dates and Almonds

This is a quick and easy Middle Eastern side dish that can be made ahead. To reheat, cover tightly and heat in a preheated 350°F (180°C) for 15 to 20 minutes, or until hot.

Barley couscous is a traditional Moroccan specialty that has only recently become available in North America. It works the same way as regular couscous, tastes delicious and is more nutritious. If you can't find it, just use regular couscous.

To cut dates easily, use scissors.

2 cups (500 mL) instant regular or barley couscous
2 cups (500 mL) boiling water
3 tbsp (45 mL) extra-virgin olive oil or butter
1 tsp (5 mL) kosher salt
Peel of 1 preserved lemon,
    or 1 tbsp (15 mL) grated lemon peel
5 dates (preferably Medjool), pitted and cut up
½ cup (125 mL) chopped toasted almonds
2 tbsp (25 mL) chopped fresh cilantro

1. Place couscous in a shallow baking dish and pour boiling water over top (if you are using barley couscous, you may need a little extra water). Stir in oil and salt. Cover tightly with foil and let stand for 10 minutes.
2. Fluff couscous with a fork and stir in preserved lemon, dates, almonds and cilantro. Taste and adjust seasonings if necessary.

MAKES 8 SERVINGS

Salad with Pomegranate Dressing

As long as you have a jar of pomegranate molasses on hand, you can prepare an exotic salad in a couple of minutes. Use more lemon juice if you don't have the pomegranate molasses. Add avocado, roasted squash or roasted red peppers if you wish.

12 cups (3 L) salad greens
⅓ cup (75 mL) shelled pumpkin seeds or walnuts, lightly toasted
1 tbsp (15 mL) chopped fresh mint
Rose petals (organically grown), optional

POMEGRANATE DRESSING
1 tbsp (15 mL) pomegranate molasses
1 tbsp (15 mL) lemon juice or sherry vinegar
1 tbsp (15 mL) brown sugar
¾ tsp (4 mL) kosher salt
⅓ cup (75 mL) extra-virgin olive oil

1. Place salad greens in a large serving bowl and toss with pumpkin seeds, mint and rose petals, if using.
2. To prepare dressing, in a bowl, whisk pomegranate molasses with lemon juice, sugar and salt. Whisk in oil. Taste and adjust seasonings if necessary.
3. Toss salad with dressing just before serving.

MAKES 8 SERVINGS

Individual Halvah Soufflés

This is a fabulous dessert made with halvah, a delicious confection made from tahina (sesame seed paste). The soufflés can be assembled ahead and baked just before serving. Dust them with icing sugar and serve with date honey or chocolate sauce (page 201).

8 egg yolks
½ cup (125 mL) granulated sugar
½ cup (125 mL) milk or soy milk
12 oz (375 g) halvah, chopped
1 tbsp (15 mL) vanilla paste or pure vanilla extract
6 egg whites (¾ cup/175 mL)
2 tbsp (25 mL) granulated sugar

1. Beat egg yolks with ½ cup (125 mL) sugar in a bowl set over a pot of simmering water. Beat in milk. Cook for about 5 minutes, or until mixture is thick. Remove from heat. Stir in halvah and vanilla. Cool until lukewarm.

2. In a large bowl, beat egg whites until opaque. Beat in 2 tbsp (25 mL) sugar and continue to beat until firm but not stiff. Stir one-quarter of egg whites into halvah mixture. Fold two mixtures together.

3. Spoon mixture into small ramekins that have been buttered or sprayed with nonstick cooking spray and dusted with granulated sugar. Place ramekins on a baking sheet and bake in a preheated 350°F (180°C) oven for 12 to 15 minutes, or until soufflés are puffed and browned. Serve immediately.

MAKES 8 TO 10 SERVINGS

Date Honey

You can buy date honey in Middle Eastern stores (it looks like dark honey), or you can make it yourself (it will look more like date puree).

In a saucepan, combine 2½ cups (625 mL) pitted dates, 4 cups (1 L) water, ½ cinnamon stick, 1 star anise and 2 whole cloves. Bring to a boil. Reduce heat and simmer, uncovered, for 1 hour. Discard spices and puree date mixture. Return to saucepan and cook very gently for 45 to 60 minutes, or until thickened.

Makes about 1½ cups (375 mL).

100-mile diet dinner

SERVES 8

Although I always buy local meat and poultry, and I try to buy local produce as much as possible, I had no idea what I was in for when I agreed to host James MacKinnon and Alisa Smith (authors of *The 100-Mile Diet: A Year of Local Eating*) at my book club. We take a lot for granted when we use rice, sugar, olive oil and lemons, for example. In the end even James and Alisa found it hard to believe that we had cooked the entire dinner with local ingredients (though I have to admit we extended the range to 150 miles at times).

It was an eye-opening exercise. We managed to chase down local canola and soybean oil, learned that the largest salt mine in the world is in Goderich, and found a great flour mill in Arva—all close to Toronto.

The challenges of eating locally vary depending on where you live. Everyone has to make compromises, and don't forget, "almost" all local is good, too.

My biggest tip for cooking locally? Keep your ingredient lists short. Or have a 100-mile potluck dinner, so everyone can share the fun and aggravation!

Except for the kale, which should be sauteed just before serving, this entire menu can be prepared ahead.

Apple Cranberry Sangria

Ontario produces a lot of cranberries. You can also find local apple brandy and sparkling wine here, but this recipe can be adapted depending on what is available in your area.

For a non-alcoholic version, omit the apple brandy and use soda water or ginger ale instead of wine.

2 cups (500 mL) apple juice or apple cider
2 cups (500 mL) cranberry juice
¼ cup (50 mL) apple brandy, optional
¼ cup (50 mL) honey
1 cup (250 mL) fresh or frozen cranberries
3 cups (750 mL) sparkling white wine

1. In a pitcher, combine apple juice, cranberry juice and brandy, if using.
2. Stir in honey and cranberries. Refrigerate until ready to serve.
3. Add sparkling wine and serve over ice.

MAKES 8 SERVINGS

Smoked Trout Spread

In southern Ontario, trout is the only local fish that is commercially available year round, although fresh whitefish, pike, perch and pickerel are also sometimes sold (Rick Blackwood of Mike's in Toronto's St. Lawrence Market is a great source of information about local fish).

We made our own mayonnaise using local oil, but you could use yogurt, instead. Serve this with bread or crackers.

8 oz (250 g) smoked trout, bones and skin removed
1 stalk celery, finely chopped
2 tbsp (25 mL) chopped fresh chives
2 tbsp (25 mL) chopped fresh dill
½ cup (125 mL) mayonnaise or yogurt, approx.
Salt to taste
Apple cider vinegar to taste
Sprigs fresh dill or chives for garnish

1. In a food processor, combine trout, celery, chives, dill and ¼ cup (50 mL) mayonnaise. Process on/off until mixture just holds together, adding more mayonnaise if necessary. Add salt and/or apple cider vinegar to taste.
2. Serve garnished with fresh dill.

MAKES ABOUT 1½ CUPS (375 ML)

Mayonnaise

In a food processor, combine 2 egg yolks, 1 tbsp (15 mL) apple cider vinegar, 1 tsp (5 mL) dry mustard and ½ tsp (2 mL) salt. With machine running, very slowly add 1¼ cups (300 mL) vegetable oil through feed tube. (You can also do this in a bowl with a whisk, adding the oil drop by drop at first and graduating to a thin stream.)

Makes about 1½ cups (375 mL).

Braised Lamb Shanks with Wine and Herbs

Although this recipe contains tons of garlic, the long cooking time makes it unexpectedly mild and sweet. You can serve the lamb shanks on the bone or remove the meat in chunks (to avoid scaring guests with what looks like a huge hunk of meat).

Peel fresh tomatoes by cutting out the core, cutting a cross on the bottom and blanching for 20 seconds in boiling water. Cool under cold water and remove the skins, or use a soft skin peeler.

> 8 lamb shanks, trimmed
> 1 tbsp (15 mL) salt
> 2 tbsp (25 mL) vegetable oil
> 3 onions, coarsely chopped
> 12 cloves garlic, peeled
> 2 cups (500 mL) dry red wine
> 2 lb (1 kg) fresh tomatoes, peeled and chopped,
>   or 1 28-oz (796 mL) can plum tomatoes, with juices
> 1 tbsp (15 mL) fresh thyme, or ½ tsp (2 mL) dried
> 2 tbsp (25 mL) coarsely chopped fresh parsley, optional

1. Pat lamb dry and sprinkle with salt.
2. Heat oil in a Dutch oven over medium-high heat. Brown lamb well on all sides, in batches if necessary (this will take about 10 to 15 minutes). Remove from pan.
3. Add onions and garlic to pan and cook for a few minutes. Add wine, bring to a boil and cook for 5 to 8 minutes, or until liquid is reduced by about half.
4. Add tomatoes and thyme and bring to a boil, breaking up tomatoes with a spoon. Return shanks to pan. Place parchment paper directly on surface of lamb. Cover with lid and cook in a preheated 350°F (180°C) oven for 2½ to 3 hours, or until meat is very tender.
5. Remove shanks from pan. Skim any fat from surface of sauce and discard. Puree sauce in a food processor or blender and return sauce to pan.
6. Remove lamb from bones in large chunks and return to sauce. Heat thoroughly. Garnish with parsley, if using.

MAKES 8 SERVINGS

Roasted Carrots

For a beautiful presentation, cut the carrots in long pieces and arrange on bed of parsley.

    4 lb (2 kg) carrots, peeled and cut in half lengthwise
    2 tbsp (25 mL) vegetable oil
    2 tsp (10 mL) salt
    2 tbsp (25 mL) fresh thyme
    1 tbsp (15 mL) honey

1. On a parchment-lined baking sheet, combine carrots, oil, salt, thyme and honey.
2. Roast in a preheated 400°F (200°C) for 30 to 40 minutes, or until caramelized and tender.

MAKES 8 SERVINGS

Potato Gnocchi

Even though gnocchi are Italian (Biba Caggiano taught me how to make the best gnocchi ever), this is a great recipe to include in a local dinner. Use an old-fashioned food mill or ricer for perfectly smooth mashed potatoes. You could also make this using half celeriac, squash or sweet potatoes.

> 2 lb (1 kg) baking potatoes (about 4)
> 1 tbsp (15 mL) salt
> 1½ cups (375 mL) all-purpose flour
> ¼ cup (50 mL) butter or vegetable oil
> 6 fresh sage leaves, shredded
> Salt to taste

1. Bake potatoes in a preheated 400°F (200°C) oven for 1 hour, or until very tender. Cut into quarters and cool slightly. Peel and put through a food mill or ricer. Stir in salt.
2. While potatoes are still warm, knead in flour ½ cup (125 mL) at a time. Knead until dough is only slightly sticky.
3. Divide dough into four pieces and roll into ropes about ¾ inch (2 cm) thick. Cut into 1-inch (2.5 cm) pieces and roll each piece along the tines of a fork (to create indentations to hold the sauce).
4. Place gnocchi on a baking sheet lined with a floured tea towel and refrigerate for up to a day.
5. Bring a large pot of salted water to a boil. Add gnocchi and cook for about 3 minutes, or until they all come to the surface and water returns to a boil. Cook for 2 minutes longer. Drain well.
6. Toss immediately with butter, sage and salt.

MAKES **8** SERVINGS

Sautéed Kale

Kale is so curly and beautiful that for a long time people used to line fruit and vegetable platters with it instead of eating it. But when "bitter greens" became popular for health reasons, everyone started to look at kale in a new way. When I serve this at home my family usually says, "Hmm, it's really good, but a little bitter," and I remember that's what we used to say about Belgian endive, arugula, radicchio, Swiss chard and rapini.

> 2 bunches kale, roughly chopped (about 8 cups / 2 L)
> 2 tbsp (25 mL) vegetable oil
> 3 cloves garlic, finely chopped
> 1 tsp (5 mL) salt

1. Wash kale well and leave a little water clinging to leaves.
2. Heat oil in a large skillet over medium-high heat. Add garlic and cook for a few minutes, or until tender but not brown.
3. Add kale and cook, stirring, for about 10 minutes, or until wilted and tender. Season with salt.

MAKES 8 SERVINGS

Caramelized Apple Crêpes with Maple Syrup

Local maple syrup and apples are legendary in Ontario. If you don't have maple syrup, use honey, which is available locally in most places. I find most apples are good for cooking if they are very apple-y and not too tart or crisp.

    2 tbsp (25 mL) butter or vegetable oil
    6 cooking apples, peeled, cored and cut in wedges
    ½ cup (125 mL) maple syrup
    10 cooked crêpes (pages 272–273)

1. Heat butter in a large heavy skillet over medium-high heat. Add apples and cook, stirring, for about 5 minutes, or until lightly browned.
2. Add maple syrup and bring to a boil. Reduce heat and cook for 5 to 7 minutes, or until apples are tender and caramelized.
3. To assemble crêpes, place crêpes, nicest side down, on a work surface. Divide apple mixture among crêpes. Roll up and place on a parchment-lined baking sheet.
4. Before serving, warm crêpes in a preheated 350°F (180°C) oven for 5 to 10 minutes.

MAKES 8 TO 10 SERVINGS

WHISKEY SOURS

LENTIL SOUP WITH CARAMELIZED ONIONS

FRIDAY NIGHT BRISKET

PIEROGI WITH POTATOES AND CARAMELIZED ONIONS

ROASTED BROCCOLI

ANNA'S HOUSE SALAD

JENNY SOLTZ'S CHALLAH

PATTI'S APPLE COBBLER

nostalgia dinner

SERVES 8

Brisket and an apple dessert will always smell like Friday night dinner to me. That's the smell I remember the most from my mother's kitchen. Once in a while I take this brisket dinner to a friend or relative, and then even my car smells like Friday night dinner. It almost makes me want to become a Friday night dinner caterer!

This is a fusion dinner that combines traditional Middle Eastern (Sephardic) and Eastern European (Ashkenazi) dishes.

Baking bread is fun, so I encourage you to make your own, but many bakeries also produce excellent challah (sometimes it is just called egg bread).

Except for the final tossing of the salad, this entire menu can be prepared ahead. Reheat the brisket, pierogi and broccoli before serving. Bake or reheat during dinner.

Whiskey Sours

Whiskey sours are so old-fashioned that they are in style again. They taste grown-up and delicious. When you order one at a restaurant or bar they often make the drink with bar mix, but if you make your own you'll have a new standard to compare it to.

You can also make this in larger quantities in a pitcher.

I always make a lot of sugar syrup as it keeps in the refrigerator indefinitely and it is great to have on hand.

¼ cup (50 mL) rye whiskey
2 tbsp (25 mL) lemon juice
2 tbsp (25 mL) sugar syrup
Ice

1. Combine whiskey, lemon juice and sugar syrup in a cocktail shaker with ice. Shake 10 times and strain into a martini glass or cocktail glass. I like it served on ice.

MAKES 1 DRINK

Sugar Syrup
In a saucepan, combine 2 cups (500 mL) water and 2 cups (500 mL) granulated sugar. Bring to a boil. Cool and refrigerate.

Makes about 3 cups (750 mL).

Lentil Soup with Caramelized Onions

I like to use red lentils in soup because they dissolve and thicken, whereas green lentils hold their shape. This soup also tastes great with cilantro pesto (page 48) swirled through it, garnished with tahina sauce (page 194) or sprinkled with chopped toasted hazelnuts or dukkah, an Egyptian mixture of nuts and seeds.

  1 tbsp (15 mL) vegetable oil
  2 large onions, chopped
  1 clove garlic, finely chopped
  1 jalapeño, seeded and chopped
  1 stalk celery, diced
  1 carrot, diced
  1 tsp (5 mL) ground cumin
  1 cup (250 mL) dried red lentils, rinsed
  6 cups (1.5 L) water
  1 tsp (5 mL) kosher salt
  ¼ tsp (1 mL) pepper
  2 tbsp (25 mL) lemon juice, optional
  ¼ cup (50 mL) chopped fresh cilantro

1. Heat oil in a large saucepan over medium-high heat. Add onions and cook for 20 to 25 minutes, or until very brown and caramelized. Reserve half the onions for garnish.
2. Add garlic, jalapeño, celery and carrot to onions remaining in saucepan and cook gently for 5 minutes. Add cumin and cook until fragrant, about 30 seconds.
3. Add lentils, water, salt and pepper. Bring to a boil. Reduce heat and simmer for 25 to 30 minutes, or until lentils are very tender and mixture is thick. If soup becomes too thick, add a little stock or water. If it is not thick enough, puree all or part of it (soup will also thicken if made ahead and refrigerated). Taste and adjust seasonings if necessary.
4. Add lemon juice, if using. Serve soup sprinkled with reserved onions and cilantro.

MAKES 8 SERVINGS

Friday Night Brisket

My mother made brisket for Friday night dinner more often than any other meat. My father loved it. She would sprinkle the brisket with a packet of onion soup mix, which was a very common thing to do at that time. It was great.

Since then, everyone has come to love brisket. Southern-style barbecue has become really popular, and today chefs are serving brisket shredded over poutine, stuffed into baby roasted potatoes, on pasta and in ravioli (great ways to use leftovers that my mother never dreamed of but would have loved!).

Brisket takes a long time to cook, but it is the easiest thing to make. It's also the perfect make-ahead dish, because it's easier to cut into nice slices when it's cold. If you make it a day or two ahead, refrigerate the meat and juices separately. Before serving, slice the brisket and reassemble it in a large shallow baking dish. Remove the solidified fat from the top of the juices and then spoon the juices over the meat (don't worry if the juices are jellied). Cover tightly, place on a baking sheet to catch any drips and reheat in a 350°F (180°C) oven for 40 to 50 minutes, or until hot and bubbling. (You can also freeze it.)

I like to buy a double brisket because it is juicier, but if you prefer leaner meat, buy a single brisket, or ask the butcher for a brisket that has a section of each—that way everyone will be happy.

 1 6-lb (3 kg) double brisket
 1 tbsp (15 mL) Dijon mustard
 1 tbsp (15 mL) kosher salt
 1 tbsp (15 mL) pepper
 1 tbsp (15 mL) paprika
 1 head garlic, separated into cloves and peeled
 3 large onions, sliced
 1 cup (250 mL) Port
 2 cups (500 mL) dry red wine
 1 cup (250 mL) beef stock, chicken stock or water, approx.

1. Spread brisket with mustard and sprinkle with salt, pepper and paprika.
2. Place garlic and most of onions in bottom of a Dutch oven. Place brisket on top. Top with remaining onions. Add Port, wine and stock (liquid should come at least halfway up sides of brisket). Bring to a boil. Place parchment paper directly on top of brisket. Cover tightly with a lid or foil.
3. Roast in a preheated 350°F (180°C) oven for at least 3 to 4 hours, or until meat is fork-tender (don't worry if it takes longer). Check every hour or so to make sure there is at least an inch of liquid in pan (add water if necessary).
4. Remove lid and paper and continue to cook meat until browned, about 30 minutes.
5. Remove brisket to a carving board. Strain liquid if you wish. Remove as much fat as you can. Carve brisket and serve with juices and onions.

MAKES 8 TO 10 SERVINGS

Shepherd's Pie

I like to make shepherd's pie with leftover brisket, shortribs (page 8) or lamb shanks (page 78). This is a great time to improvise. You can shred the meat so it is still in pieces, or chop it all up in the food processor. Add the brisket juices to moisten the meat, but if there isn't a lot of juice left over, add some tomato sauce. Add diced leftover cooked vegetables or some frozen corn, peas and carrots, or even edamame. For the topping I use leftover mashed potatoes, sweet potatoes or any mashed root vegetable. You can also use polenta (page 22) or cornbread batter (page 278).

I usually use about 3 cups (750 mL) meat mixture, ½ to 1 cup (125 to 250 mL) sauce, up to 2 cups (500 mL) vegetables and 2 to 3 cups (500 to 750 mL) mash for a 13- x 9-inch (3 L) baking dish. Place on a baking sheet and bake, uncovered, in a preheated 350°F (180°C) oven for 35 to 45 minutes, or until bubbling.

Makes 8 servings.

Pierogi with Potatoes and Caramelized Onions

Pierogi can be a meal in themselves. They are also delicious as a first course or served as a side dish with roasted meat or chicken. There are many different stuffings, but I love potatoes and onions the best. Serve with or without sour cream. I usually make lots and freeze (uncooked) what I don't need.

Traditionally pierogi have thick, doughy skins, but I like them made with Chinese dumpling wrappers or pasta dough, as they are lighter (and you can eat more!).

1½ lb (750 g) Yukon Gold potatoes, peeled and cut in chunks
¼ cup (50 mL) vegetable oil
6 onions, sliced
Kosher salt to taste
¼ cup (50 mL) butter or vegetable oil
1 egg
2 tsp (10 mL) kosher salt
¼ tsp (1 mL) pepper
70 round 3-inch (7.5 cm) dumpling wrappers (about 1 lb/500 g)

1. In a saucepan, cover potatoes with cold water, bring to a boil and cook for 30 minutes, or until very tender.
2. Meanwhile, heat oil in a large, deep skillet over medium-high heat. Add onions. Do not stir until they start to brown. Keep cooking until brown and tender, about 20 minutes. (If pan is dry, add a little more oil.) Season with salt.
3. Remove ½ cup (125 mL) browned onions from skillet and chop.
4. Drain potatoes well and mash with chopped onions, butter, egg, salt and pepper.
5. Lay dumpling wrappers (about 12 at a time) on work surface. Place about 1½ tsp (7 mL) potato filling on each wrapper. Dab a little water around edge of half the wrapper and press edges together well. Arrange on parchment-lined baking sheets. Repeat until all wrappers or potatoes are used.
6. Cook pierogi in 2 batches in a large pot of boiling salted water. Once they rise to the surface, cook for 5 minutes, or until very tender.
7. Heat remaining onions in skillet. Drain pierogi and add. Heat thoroughly before serving.

MAKES ABOUT 70 PIEROGI

Roasted Broccoli

This sounds so easy but tastes so good. When broccoli is roasted, the flavor intensifies. You can make this just with the florets, but my daughter only likes the stalks (she says when the florets are slightly crispy they taste too much like "trees").

Serve this as a side dish, a salad, tossed with pasta, added to a pasta casserole (like macaroni and cheese), pureed with chicken stock to make an intensely flavored soup or used in sandwiches (like grilled cheese) and wraps.

If you make this ahead, reheat it in a 350°F (180°C) oven for 10 minutes. It can also be served at room temperature.

2 cloves garlic, minced
3 tbsp (45 mL) extra-virgin olive oil
1 tsp (5 mL) kosher salt
3 lb (1.5 kg) broccoli, trimmed and cut in 1-inch (2.5 cm) pieces

1. In a large bowl, combine garlic, oil and salt. Add broccoli and toss. Spread on a parchment-lined baking sheet.
2. Roast in a preheated 400°F (200°C) oven for 20 to 25 minutes, or until tender and lightly browned.

MAKES 8 SERVINGS

Anna's House Salad

My daughter, Anna, never liked salads. No matter how many she tasted (or didn't taste) at home, in fancy restaurants, at university or at friends' houses, she always resisted. Then one day she came home and said she had tasted a sweetish Asian dressing on iceberg lettuce and she liked it. Now she has seconds. (Note to mothers of fussy eaters—say nothing. I know it's hard but one day they will have an epiphany.)

This dressing tastes good on everything from plain iceberg lettuce to chicken salad. It will keep in the refrigerator for up to a week.

> 3 tbsp (45 mL) seasoned rice vinegar
> 1 clove garlic, minced
> ½ tsp (2 mL) kosher salt
> 1 tbsp (15 mL) soy sauce
> 1 tbsp (15 mL) honey
> ¼ tsp (1 mL) roasted sesame oil, optional
> ⅓ cup (75 mL) vegetable oil
> 12 cups (3 L) torn Romaine hearts or iceberg lettuce

1. In a bowl, combine vinegar, garlic, salt, soy sauce, honey and sesame oil, if using. Whisk in oil.
2. Just before serving, toss lettuce with dressing to taste.

MAKES 8 SERVINGS

Jenny Soltz's Challah

I have no idea whether this is my grandmother's actual recipe, but I like to think it is. My grandparents lived in Grand Valley, Ontario, had eleven children (my mom was number ten) and were very poor. My grandmother kept her family in bread all winter by winning first place in the county fair with her amazing challahs. The prize was flour.

Although challah is the traditional bread to welcome Shabbat, you don't have to be Jewish to love it. Challah is more than a pretty face; it's a fragrant, sweet-tasting loaf with a cakelike texture. It has transcended its roots and is now sold everywhere (upscale restaurants that serve brunch wouldn't use anything else in their French toast).

You can sprinkle the unbaked challah with poppy seeds, sesame seeds, salt, streusel topping or, my new favorite, za'atar (page 7)—a tip from my Israeli friend and colleague Judy Stacey Goldman—but it is also great just glazed with beaten egg.

Braid the bread in three, four or six strands, make one huge loaf, two regular loaves or smaller loaves or buns. The smaller the loaves, the less time they will take to bake.

My grandmother could never have done this, but a really good tip is to use a meat thermometer if you are not sure the challah is cooked through.

> 1 tsp (5 mL) granulated sugar
>
> 1½ cups (375 mL) warm water, divided
>
> 2 tbsp (25 mL) dry yeast (2 packages)
>
> ½ cup (125 mL) vegetable oil
>
> ½ cup (125 mL) granulated sugar
>
> 1 tbsp (15 mL) kosher salt
>
> 4 eggs, lightly beaten
>
> 5 to 7 cups (1.25 to 1.75 L) all-purpose flour (or part whole wheat flour)

1. In a large bowl, dissolve 1 tsp (5 mL) sugar in ½ cup (125 mL) warm water (about 110°F/43°C) and sprinkle yeast over top. Let stand for 10 minutes, or until yeast bubbles up and mixture doubles in volume.

2. Meanwhile, in a separate bowl, combine remaining 1 cup (250 mL) warm water with oil, ½ cup (125 mL) sugar and salt. (Or, heat water in a saucepan and stir in oil, sugar and salt until dissolved.)

3. Reserve (refrigerate) 2 tbsp (25 mL) beaten eggs for glaze. Add remaining eggs to liquid.

4. Stir down yeast and stir into egg mixture.

5. Gradually stir in enough flour to make a soft, moist dough that is not too sticky. On a floured surface, knead dough, adding flour as necessary to form a soft dough. (Dough should feel like a woman's inner thigh. No one believes I really tell people this but it is true!) Knead for about 10 minutes by hand. Add extra flour very gradually. It is always better to have a moist dough than a dry one. (This can also be done in a mixer. Knead only for 5 minutes and be extra careful not to add too much flour.)

6. Place dough in an oiled bowl and turn to coat with oil. Cover bowl with plastic wrap and then with a tea towel. Set in a warm place and let rise until doubled—about 1 hour.

7. Punch dough down and divide in half. Divide each half into three strands and roll into ropes about 14 inches (35 cm) long. Braid three strands together and turn ends under. Place braided loaves on two parchment-lined baking sheets. Cover loosely with oiled plastic wrap and let rise for 1 hour, or until doubled.

8. Brush challahs gently with reserved egg mixture. Bake in a preheated 350°F (180°C) oven for 25 to 30 minutes, or until a meat thermometer inserted into bread reads 195°F (90°C). Cool on a rack.

MAKES 2 LARGE CHALLAHS

French Toast Casserole

A cross between French toast and bread pudding, this is a great way to use up leftover challah. My friend Helen Kirzner served this incredible dish for brunch one Sunday and I have been making it ever since. Serve it for brunch or dessert on its own, or with ice cream, yogurt, additional maple syrup, caramelized apples, bananas or sliced berries.

In a large bowl, combine 7 eggs, 2½ cups (625 mL) milk, 1½ tsp (7 mL) vanilla paste or extract and 1¼ lb (625 g) challah cut in 1-inch (2.5 cm) chunks (about 8 cups/2 L). Cover and refrigerate overnight.

Transfer to a buttered 13- x 9-inch (3 L) baking dish.

In a small bowl, combine ½ cup (125 mL) melted butter, ¾ cup (175 mL) brown sugar and 2 tbsp (25 mL) maple syrup. Drizzle over bread.

Bake in a preheated 350°F (180°C) oven for 40 to 45 minutes, or until puffed and browned. Cool for 5 minutes before serving.

Makes 8 servings.

Patti's Apple Cobbler

One of my best friends, Patti Linzon, entertains beautifully. She made me this amazing apple cobbler, and now I make it all the time. The topping is quite different—Patti adapted it from a recipe she found in Cape Cod, and I adapted it from her version. I like to make it with a combination of Spy and McIntosh apples, as the Spys keep their shape and the Macs kind of melt.

You can make this ahead and serve it at room temperature or reheat it. I like to bake it during dinner—the marvelous aromas permeate the house while you are eating. Serve it plain or with ice cream or non-dairy frozen dessert.

8 apples, peeled and thickly sliced
1 tbsp (15 mL) ground cinnamon
¼ tsp (1 mL) ground nutmeg
½ cup (125 mL) granulated sugar

TOPPING
1½ cups (375 mL) all-purpose flour
¾ cup (175 mL) granulated sugar
¾ cup (175 mL) brown sugar
¾ tsp (4 mL) baking powder
Pinch kosher salt
2 eggs, beaten
½ cup (125 mL) melted butter or vegetable oil
2 tbsp (25 mL) coarse sugar, optional

1. Place apples in a large bowl and toss with cinnamon, nutmeg and granulated sugar. Place in a 13- x 9-inch (3 L) baking dish.
2. To prepare topping, in a large bowl, combine flour, granulated sugar, brown sugar, baking powder and salt. Make a well in center. Add beaten eggs.
3. With your fingers (or a large fork), combine eggs with flour mixture until crumbly. Sprinkle over apples. Drizzle with melted butter. Sprinkle with coarse sugar, if using.
4. Bake in a preheated 350°F (180°C) oven for 45 to 55 minutes, or until apples are very tender.

MAKES 8 TO 10 SERVINGS

middle eastern dinner

SERVES 8

I love the idea of bringing a huge platter to the table with the complete main course on it, and this fattah is one of those stunning platters. Although you can make the main course ahead and reheat it in a casserole dish, when you serve it on a platter—usually too round and large to fit in most ovens—it is a beautiful thing.

   Much of this menu can be prepared ahead, including the hummos, tomato salad, dessert and sauces for the main course. Assemble the chicken cigars a few days ahead and freeze them; they can be baked directly from the frozen state just before serving.

Matboucha (Moroccan Cooked Tomato Salad)

This is a delicious dip that I often serve along with an eggplant dip (page 180) and hummos. Peel the red peppers and tomatoes with a soft skin peeler to eliminate broiling and boiling.

    This cooked salad was introduced to me by Rhonda Caplan, who worked with me at the cooking school for many years. She had it often in restaurants in Montreal, where there is a large Moroccan population. Although I have since had it many times in Israel, this is still the best version I have tasted. It also freezes well. Serve it with grilled pita (pages 226–227) or crackers, or as a sauce with pasta, meatloaf or chicken.

> 1 tbsp (15 mL) extra-virgin olive oil
> 6 cloves garlic, finely chopped
> 2 jalapeños, seeded and chopped
> 4 sweet red peppers, peeled, seeded and diced
> 3 lb (1.5 kg) plum tomatoes, peeled, seeded and chopped,
>   or 2 28-oz (796 mL) cans plum tomatoes, drained and chopped
> 1 tsp (5 mL) kosher salt

1. Heat oil in a large, deep skillet over medium heat. Add garlic and jalapeños and cook gently for a few minutes, or until soft and fragrant.
2. Add red peppers, tomatoes and salt and cook for 20 to 30 minutes, or until thickened. Taste and adjust seasonings if necessary.

MAKES 3 CUPS (750 ML)

Creamy Hummos

This is a casual-style hummos, common in the Middle East but not so much here. My Israeli friends say it is sometimes served with some of the freshly cooked warm chickpeas mashed or pureed into the tahina and the rest of the chickpeas just folded in.

Serve it with grilled pita (pages 226–227), challah (pages 94–95) or mini pita breads to scoop up the chickpeas.

½ cup (125 mL) tahina
3 tbsp (45 mL) lemon juice
½ cup (125 mL) water
½ tsp (2 mL) kosher salt
1 jalapeño, seeded and finely chopped
1 clove garlic, minced
¼ tsp (1 mL) ground cumin, optional
2 cups (500 mL) cooked or canned chickpeas
2 tbsp (25 mL) chopped fresh cilantro
1 tbsp (15 mL) chopped fresh mint, optional
2 tbsp (25 mL) extra-virgin olive oil
½ tsp (2 mL) harissa, hot red pepper sauce or aleppo pepper

1. In a bowl, whisk together tahina, lemon juice and water. Mixture should be smooth. Stir in salt, jalapeño, garlic and cumin, if using.
2. Add chickpeas, cilantro and mint, if using. Taste and adjust seasonings if necessary. Spoon into a shallow dish.
3. In a small bowl, combine oil and harissa and drizzle over hummos.

MAKES ABOUT 2 CUPS (500 ML)

Moroccan Chicken Cigars

This is a take-off on B'stilla, the famous Moroccan chicken and phyllo pie sprinkled with cinnamon and icing sugar. You can make these ahead and freeze them baked or unbaked. In both cases, bake them from the frozen state—reheat frozen baked pastries for 20 to 30 minutes and frozen unbaked pastries for 40 to 50 minutes.

Israeli chef Ariel Porat cooked these at a dinner in honor of Tu Bi'shevat, a festival celebrating trees and the land of Israel. The Canadian arm of the Jewish National Fund brought him to Canada to show people how delicious Israeli food can be. He served these in shooter glasses with a little cinnamon sugar in the bottom for dipping.

You could also use ground beef instead of chicken. Or, for a vegetarian version, use curried lentil filling (page 123).

1 tbsp (15 mL) extra-virgin olive oil
1 small onion, finely chopped
3 cloves garlic, finely chopped
1 tsp (5 mL) ground cumin
1 tsp (5 mL) paprika
¼ tsp (1 mL) cayenne
¼ tsp (1 mL) ground cinnamon
1 lb (500 g) ground or chopped chicken
1 egg, beaten
1 tbsp (15 mL) honey
1 tsp (5 mL) harissa or hot red pepper sauce
Salt and pepper to taste
12 sheets phyllo pastry
½ cup (125 mL) extra-virgin olive oil
¾ cup (175 mL) panko or dry breadcrumbs
2 tbsp (25 mL) sesame seeds

CINNAMON SUGAR
¼ cup (50 mL) coarse sugar
¼ tsp (1 mL) ground cinnamon

1. Heat oil in a large skillet over medium-high heat. Add onion and garlic and cook for a few minutes, or until tender and lightly browned.

2. Add cumin, paprika, cayenne and cinnamon and cook for 30 seconds, or until fragrant.

3. Add chicken and cook until chicken loses its raw appearance, about 5 minutes. Remove from heat. Stir in egg, honey and harissa. Season to taste with salt and pepper. Cool.

4. Remove phyllo from package just before using. Cut stack of twelve in half crosswise. Cover with plastic wrap and a damp tea towel. Place oil and breadcrumbs in two separate small dishes.

5. To make cigars (I usually make two at a time, keeping rest of phyllo covered), brush piece of phyllo with oil and sprinkle with breadcrumbs.

6. Form about 1 tbsp (15 mL) filling into a log about 6 inches (15 cm) long. Place on center bottom part of strip of phyllo. Fold edges over filling and roll up tightly into a cigar shape. Arrange on a parchment-lined baking sheet. Brush top with oil and sprinkle with sesame seeds. Repeat until all filling is used.

7. Bake in a preheated 350°F (180°C) oven for 20 minutes, or until browned.

8. In a small bowl, combine sugar and cinnamon. Place a bit in shooter glasses and stand a cigar up in each. Or place cigars on a serving platter with cinnamon sugar in a little dish for dipping.

MAKES 24 CIGARS

Bonnie's Chicken Fattah

This is my version of fattah, a Middle Eastern layered dish that is incredibly delicious—much more than the sum of its parts. I start with mujedrah (rice and lentils with browned onions) and layer it with grilled chicken, Moroccan tomato sauce and tahina. The result is a flavorful, attractive and exotic main course that is perfect for sharing.

All the components of the dish can be made ahead. The mujedrah is delicious as a main course or side dish; the chicken thighs can be served on skewers as appetizers with either the tomato sauce or tahina. The tomato sauce can also be used on meatballs and meatloaf instead of regular tomato sauce, and the tahina can be served with any roasted meat or fish.

For a vegetarian dish, use four Asian eggplants (sliced lengthwise) or eight portobello mushroom caps instead of the chicken.

MUJEDRAH
2 tbsp (25 mL) extra-virgin olive oil
3 large onions, thinly sliced
2 cups (500 mL) mixed brown rice, rinsed if necessary
1 cup (250 mL) green lentils, rinsed
5 cups (1.25 L) water
2 tsp (10 mL) kosher salt

CHICKEN
2 tbsp (25 mL) extra-virgin olive oil
2 tsp (10 mL) kosher salt
2 tsp (10 mL) sumac or grated lemon peel
2 tsp (10 mL) minced garlic
4 lb (2 kg) boneless, skinless chicken thighs or breasts, or a combination

MOROCCAN TOMATO SAUCE
2 tbsp (25 mL) extra-virgin olive oil
1 onion, chopped
4 cloves garlic, chopped
1 tsp (5 mL) ground cumin (preferably toasted)
Pinch hot red pepper flakes or aleppo pepper
1 28-oz (796 mL) can plum tomatoes, with juices, pureed or chopped
1 tbsp (15 mL) honey

1 tbsp (15 mL) lemon juice
Salt and pepper to taste

TAHINA SAUCE
2 cloves garlic, peeled
⅓ cup (75 mL) tahina
¼ cup (50 mL) lemon juice
½ cup (125 mL) water
½ tsp (2 mL) hot red pepper sauce
Salt to taste

GARNISH
3 tbsp (45 mL) chopped fresh cilantro
3 tbsp (45 mL) toasted pine nuts

1. To prepare mujedrah, heat oil in a large, deep skillet over medium-high heat. Add onions and cook for 15 to 20 minutes, or until very brown, with some of onions slightly blackish in places. Remove half of onions from pan and reserve.

2. Add rice to onions in skillet and cook for a few minutes. Add lentils, water and salt and bring to a boil. Cover and cook gently for 40 to 45 minutes, or until just tender. Taste and adjust seasonings if necessary.

3. Meanwhile, to prepare chicken, combine oil, salt, sumac and garlic in a small bowl. Rub into chicken. Grill or roast chicken until cooked through and tender, about 8 to 10 minutes per side on grill or 30 to 40 minutes at 400°F (200°C).

4. Meanwhile, to prepare tomato sauce, in a large skillet, heat oil over medium heat. Add onion and garlic and cook for 5 minutes, or until tender but not brown.

5. Add cumin and hot pepper flakes and cook gently for 30 seconds. Add tomatoes and bring to a boil. Cook gently, uncovered, for 15 to 20 minutes, or until thick. Season with honey, lemon juice, salt and pepper.

6. To prepare tahina sauce, in a food processor, combine garlic, tahina, lemon juice, water and hot pepper sauce until smooth. Add salt to taste.

7. To assemble, spread rice and lentils on a large platter. Arrange chicken on top. Spoon tomato sauce over chicken. Sprinkle with reserved onions, cilantro and pine nuts. Drizzle with tahina.

MAKES 8 TO 10 SERVINGS

Moroccan Fruit Salad

A stunning platter of oranges (if available, I like to use a combination of navel, blood and cara cara), grapefruit and dried fruit is great after a big dinner. It is easy to prepare and very refreshing. Orange blossom water is becoming more popular, but if you can't find it, try a Middle Eastern store. Be sure to use just a tiny bit, as a little is exotic, but more is overpowering.

My long-time friend and colleague Scott Sellers suggested grating 70 percent chocolate on top—it's a brilliant idea.

    6 large oranges (about 12 oz/375 g each)
    2 pink grapefruit (about 12 oz/375 g each)
    Few drops orange blossom water, optional
    3 dried dates, pitted and sliced
    3 dried figs, sliced
    3 dried apricots, sliced
    2 tbsp (25 mL) chopped pistachio nuts, optional
    2 tbsp (25 mL) pomegranate seeds, optional
    2 tbsp (25 mL) grated bittersweet or semisweet chocolate, optional

1. Cut tops and bottoms off oranges and grapefruit so that they can stand up on cutting board. Cut off peel from top to bottom. Slice oranges into rounds and arrange in a large shallow dish. Cut segments from grapefruit and arrange on oranges in center of dish. Save as much juice as possible; you should have about ½ cup (125 mL). (Squeeze membranes over a bowl to catch extra juices.)

2. Stir a few drops of orange blossom water, if using, into reserved juices. Drizzle over oranges and grapefruit.

3. Scatter dates, figs and apricots over citrus fruit. Sprinkle with pistachios, pomegranate seeds and chocolate, if using.

MAKES 8 SERVINGS

Chocolate-dipped Medjool Dates Stuffed with Walnuts

Buy Medjool dates for this dessert, as they are big and juicy. You'll have more chocolate than you need, but it is easier to have extra for dipping. (Refrigerate any extra for another time. If it goes streaky, don't worry—it will smooth out again when melted.) The dates can be served cold like chocolate-dipped strawberries or warm like a fondue.

This recipe can easily be doubled.

8 oz (250 g) semisweet or bittersweet chocolate, chopped
8 Medjool dates
8 walnut halves, toasted

1. Place chocolate in a bowl set over gently simmering water until chocolate has almost melted. Remove from heat and stir until chocolate melts completely.
2. Pit dates and stuff each with a walnut half. Insert a bamboo skewer into walnuts.
3. Swirl dates in chocolate and arrange on a waxed paper-lined plate. Refrigerate.

MAKES 8

Israeli Ice Cream Sundaes

On one of our culinary trips to Israel, we had lunch in a beautiful restaurant and spice market called Tavlin. After an array of delicious salads, we were served their special dessert—an outstanding ice cream sundae. Scoops of ice cream were sprinkled with shredded halvah and toasted pecans and drizzled with tahina, date honey (page 72) and jam.

Yum.

AVOCADO AND RICOTTA SPREAD

CURRIED BUTTERNUT AND PEANUT SOUP

ROASTED VEGETABLE AND CHICKPEA POTJIE

AMAZING SOUTH AFRICAN SEED BREAD

COUSCOUS WITH NUTS AND SEEDS

LAUREN'S BRAZIL NUT BISCOTTI

PAVLOVA ROLL WITH PASSIONFRUIT CREAM

south african dinner

SERVES 8

My good friend Lauren Gutter is a talented fashion designer and a wonderful cook. When she can, she assists with classes at the cooking school, adding her great sense of style to the way we serve. She is originally from South Africa, and after years of listening to her describe the country, we finally went there with our families one Christmas. It was an eye-opening trip in many ways, and now when transplanted South Africans talk about how much they miss it, I understand why. The country and the people are so beautiful, and the food is distinctive and delicious.

South Africa is especially famous for its traditional barbecues (braais), its sausages (boerewors), bobotie (a kind of spicy meat casserole) and layered stews called potjies. When I returned home, I wanted to cook my own versions of the dishes I'd had there. Here are just a few.

Everything in this vegetarian menu can be made ahead.

Avocado and Ricotta Spread

Buy avocados a few days ahead, as it is hard to find a ripe one the day you need it. (For a tip on ripening them more quickly, see page 162.) Serve with tortilla chips.

Some jalapeños are hotter than others; if yours are very hot, just use half.

1 tbsp (15 mL) lemon juice
2 cloves garlic, minced
1 tsp (5 mL) kosher salt
1 ripe avocado, peeled and diced
4 oz (125 g) ricotta cheese
1 jalapeño, seeded and finely chopped
¼ cup (50 mL) chopped fresh cilantro or shredded basil
2 tbsp (25 mL) chopped fresh chives

1. In a bowl, combine lemon juice, garlic and salt.
2. Add avocado and ricotta and mash with a potato masher, leaving mixture slightly coarse but creamy enough to hold together.
3. Stir in jalapeño, cilantro and chives. Taste and adjust seasonings if necessary.

MAKES ABOUT 2 CUPS (500 ML)

Curried Butternut and Peanut Soup

This soup may sound unusual, but it's rich and luscious, and everyone loves it. Pumpkin and butternut squash are used a lot in South Africa and can be used interchangeably.

If any guests are allergic to peanuts, just omit the nuts and peanut butter.

2 heads garlic
2 lb (1 kg) butternut squash, seeded and cut in chunks
1 onion, peeled and cut in quarters
2 tbsp (25 mL) extra-virgin olive oil
1 tsp (5 mL) kosher salt
1 tbsp (15 mL) red Thai curry paste or Indian curry paste
4 cups (1 L) vegetable stock or water
½ cup (125 mL) coconut milk
¼ cup (50 mL) peanut butter
Salt and pepper to taste

GARNISH
½ cup (125 mL) roasted peanuts, coarsely chopped
2 tbsp (25 mL) coconut milk

1. Cut top quarter off heads of garlic and wrap garlic in foil.
2. In a large bowl, toss squash and onion with oil and salt and spread on a parchment-lined baking sheet.
3. Roast garlic and vegetables in a preheated 350°F (180°C) oven for 45 minutes, or until very tender.
4. Squeeze roasted garlic into a food processor. Peel squash and add to food processor with onions and curry paste. Puree, adding a bit of stock if necessary. Transfer to a saucepan with stock (add a little extra stock if soup seems too thick). Bring to a boil, reduce heat and simmer gently for 10 minutes.
5. Add coconut milk and cook for 5 minutes. Thin peanut butter with some of soup and then stir into soup. Season to taste with salt and pepper.
6. Serve sprinkled with peanuts and drizzled with coconut milk.

MAKES 8 SERVINGS

Roasted Vegetable and Chickpea Potjie

Lauren's son Daniel loves to cook, and when he is interested in something, he becomes passionate. He is a great help at any meal, whether it is at my house, his house or cooking with friends.

Daniel came up with this version of a traditional South African potjie when Lauren needed a meatless main course for a dinner party. It is now our go-to vegetarian entree. Just delicious. Serve it over regular couscous, Israeli couscous or brown rice. Instead of the cumin, coriander, paprika, turmeric, cinnamon and chili paste, you could use 2 to 3 tbsp (25 to 45 mL) Indian curry paste.

This makes a lot, but I always make it all and freeze any extra for emergency vegetarian meals.

1 lb (500 g) small potatoes, halved or quartered
1 lb (500 g) baby carrots, cut on diagonal
1 lb (500 g) peeled butternut or buttercup squash, cut in chunks
1 sweet red pepper, peeled, seeded and cut in chunks
1 lb (500 g) Asian eggplants, cut in chunks
¼ cup (50 mL) extra-virgin olive oil, divided
1 tsp (5 mL) kosher salt
½ tsp (2 mL) pepper
1 large onion, chopped
3 cloves garlic, finely chopped
2 tbsp (25 mL) ground cumin (preferably toasted)
2 tbsp (25 mL) ground coriander
2 tbsp (25 mL) smoked paprika
1 tbsp (15 mL) ground turmeric
½ tsp (2 mL) ground cinnamon
¼ cup (50 mL) brown sugar
2 tsp (10 mL) hot Asian chili paste, or to taste
1 28-oz (796 mL) can plum tomatoes, with juices, chopped
2 cups (500 mL) cooked or canned chickpeas
1 cup (250 mL) vegetable stock or water
¼ cup (50 mL) chopped fresh cilantro
2 cups (500 mL) unflavored yogurt

1. In a large bowl, combine potatoes, carrots, squash, red pepper and eggplants with 2 tbsp (25 mL) oil, salt and pepper. Spread on parchment-lined baking sheets and roast in a preheated 400°F (200°C) oven for 40 minutes, or until vegetables are tender.

2. Meanwhile, heat remaining 2 tbsp (25 mL) oil in a Dutch oven over medium heat. Add onion and garlic and cook for about 5 minutes, or until tender.

3. Add cumin, coriander, paprika, turmeric, cinnamon, brown sugar and chili paste. Cook, stirring, for 2 minutes, but be careful not to burn.

4. Add tomatoes, chickpeas and stock. Bring to a boil and cook for 10 minutes.

5. Add roasted vegetables to Dutch oven and cook for 30 minutes longer. Taste and adjust seasonings if necessary.

6. Sprinkle with cilantro and serve with yogurt.

MAKES 8 TO 10 SERVINGS

Amazing South African Seed Bread

When I was in Cape Town I noticed that all kinds of seeds were used in breads, sprinkled on salads and used as a garnish on soups and wherever else possible. One bread we bought had a slightly spongy texture and contained many kinds of seeds. After trying to reproduce it without much success, I consulted Phillippa Chavitz, a prolific cookbook author and food writer who lives in Cape Town, and she sent me this sensational recipe. I love it toasted, and it tastes great with dips and spreads. It doesn't require kneading and only rises once, so it is very easy once you assemble all the ingredients.

1 tbsp (15 mL) granulated sugar

2½ cups (625 mL) warm water, divided

1 tbsp (15 mL) dry yeast (1 package)

⅓ cup (75 mL) molasses

1 tbsp (15 mL) vegetable oil

2 cups (500 mL) whole wheat flour

1 cup (250 mL) rolled oats

½ cup (125 mL) rye flour

½ cup (125 mL) wheat bran

¼ cup (50 mL) wheat germ

¼ cup (50 mL) sunflower seeds

¼ cup (50 mL) sesame seeds

¼ cup (50 mL) poppy seeds

¼ cup (50 mL) flax seeds, crushed or ground, or a combination

4 tsp (20 mL) kosher salt

3 tbsp (45 mL) seeds (any combination) for topping

1. In a small bowl or measuring cup, combine sugar and ½ cup (125 mL) warm water. Sprinkle with yeast. Let stand for 10 minutes, or until yeast bubbles up and doubles in volume.

2. Meanwhile, in a separate bowl, combine remaining 2 cups (500 mL) warm water, molasses and oil.

3. In a large bowl, combine whole wheat flour, rolled oats, rye flour, bran, wheat germ, sunflower seeds, sesame seeds, poppy seeds, flax seeds and salt.

4. When yeast has risen, stir it into water/molasses mixture. Stir wet ingredients into flour mixture. Batter should be loose.

5. Turn batter into one 10-x 6-inch (3 L) or two 8-x 4-inch (1.5 L) loaf pans that have been buttered and lined with parchment paper. Press extra seeds into top. Cover loosely with plastic wrap and let rise in a warm place for about 1 hour, or until batter has risen to top of pan.

6. Bake in a preheated 350°F (180°C) oven for 1 hour for large loaf or 45 minutes for smaller ones. A meat thermometer should register 195°F (90°C) when inserted into loaf.

MAKES ONE LARGE LOAF OR TWO SMALLER ONES

Couscous with Nuts and Seeds

Here's a tasty couscous full of crunch.

2 tbsp (25 mL) extra-virgin olive oil
1 onion, chopped
2 cloves garlic, finely chopped
1 ½ cups (375 mL) vegetable stock or chicken stock
1 ½ cups (375 mL) instant couscous
Salt and pepper to taste
½ cup (125 mL) sliced toasted almonds
½ cup (125 mL) coarsely chopped toasted hazelnuts
¼ cup (50 mL) shelled pumpkin seeds, toasted
¼ cup (50 mL) sunflower seeds, toasted
2 tbsp (25 mL) sesame seeds, toasted
2 tbsp (25 mL) chopped fresh cilantro
2 tbsp (25 mL) butter, cut in bits, optional

1. Heat oil in a large saucepan over medium heat. Add onion and garlic and cook gently, without browning, for 5 to 10 minutes, or until tender.
2. Add stock and bring to a boil.
3. Stir in couscous. Remove from heat. Cover pan tightly with foil and let steam for 10 minutes. Fluff with a fork and season with salt and pepper.
4. Gently fold in nuts, seeds, cilantro and butter, if using.

MAKES 8 SERVINGS

Lauren's Brazil Nut Biscotti

This is different from most biscotti, as you bake the batter in a loaf pan and then slice the loaf paper-thin to create mosaic-like crackers. (These are also delicious served with a cheese platter.)

1½ cups (375 mL) all-purpose flour
¾ cup (175 mL) granulated sugar
½ tsp (2 mL) kosher salt
½ tsp (2 mL) baking powder
3 eggs
1 tsp (5 mL) vanilla paste or pure vanilla extract
1 lb (500 g) Brazil nuts, toasted and chopped
1 lb (500 g) dates, chopped

1. In a large bowl, combine flour, sugar, salt and baking powder.
2. In a separate bowl, combine eggs and vanilla.
3. Stir eggs, nuts and dates into flour mixture. Spoon into a 9- x 5-inch (2 L) oiled and parchment-lined loaf pan.
4. Bake in a preheated 300°F (150°C) oven for 1½ hours. Cool. Wrap well and refrigerate for a day or two for easier slicing.
5. Slice loaf as thinly as possible and place slices on a baking sheet in a single layer. Bake in a 250°F (120°C) oven for 30 to 60 minutes, or until crisp.

MAKES ABOUT 80 COOKIES

Pavlova Roll with Passionfruit Cream

When I was in South Africa, I fell in love with the zingy flavor of passionfruit (called grenadilla there). For this recipe use the puree sold in small cans in specialty shops, or buy fresh passionfruit (ripe ones are crinkled and ugly but taste amazing—cut the fruit in half and scoop out the inside). Make a delicious sangria by combining ¾ cup (175 mL) passionfruit puree, ¾ cup (175 mL) sugar syrup (page 86) and ¼ cup (50 mL) lime juice. Just before serving, add 3 cups (750 mL) sparkling white wine and serve over ice.

If you can't find passionfruit puree, use the pulp of three or four fresh passionfruit or substitute mango puree. You can also use passionfruit curd or lemon curd (page 129) instead of the whipped cream filling.

PAVLOVA

8 egg whites (about 1 cup/ 250 mL)

1¼ cups (300 mL) granulated sugar

1 tbsp (15 mL) white vinegar

1 tsp (5 mL) vanilla paste or pure vanilla extract

2 tbsp (25 mL) cornstarch

1 tbsp (15 mL) sifted icing sugar

FILLING

¾ cup (175 mL) whipping cream

1 tbsp (15 mL) vanilla paste, or 1 tsp (5 mL) pure vanilla extract plus 1 tbsp (15 mL) icing sugar

⅓ cup (75 mL) passionfruit puree

GARNISH

1 mango, peeled and cut in matchsticks

1. In a large bowl, beat egg whites until light. Slowly add sugar and beat until whites are stiff and shiny. Beat in vinegar and vanilla. Fold in cornstarch.

2. Spread meringue over a large 18- x 12-inch (45 x 30 cm) parchment-lined baking sheet. Bake in a preheated 325°F (160°C) oven for 12 to 15 minutes, or until puffy but somewhat firm. Cool.

3. Dust top of meringue with icing sugar. Run a knife around edge to loosen and then invert onto another piece of parchment.

4. For filling, in a bowl, whip cream with vanilla until light. Fold in passionfruit puree to taste. Spread over pavlova base. Roll up lengthwise. Refrigerate.

5. Slice cake and place on plates spiral side up. Garnish with fresh mango.

MAKES 8 TO 10 SERVINGS

MELTING CHEESE AND CORN QUESADILLAS
OR
CURRIED LENTIL SAMOSAS
VEGETARIAN LASAGNA CASSEROLE
NEW WAVE CAESAR SALAD
LEMON TIRAMISU

vegetarian dinner

SERVES 8 TO 10

More and more people are looking for meatless meals for all sorts of reasons—health, cost, environmental, religious or philosophical. Some are full-time vegetarians, and some only want to eat meatless meals once in a while.

This easy vegetarian menu is one that both kids and adults will love. And no one will miss the meat.

Make the samosas, lasagna, salad dressing, croutons and dessert ahead. If you are making the quesadillas, assemble them ahead but grill just before serving.

Melting Cheese and Corn Quesadillas

This is one of my most popular fallback appetizers. Everyone loves them and they are very easy to make. If you are not barbecuing, use a sandwich press, grill pan or heavy skillet. Serve them as is or with guacamole (page 152) or sour cream.

If you are grilling the corn, grill lots and freeze to use in salads, soups and risottos.

2 tbsp (25 mL) mayonnaise
1½ cups (375 mL) grated smoked mozzarella cheese
1 tsp (5 mL) pureed chipotles, or 1 jalapeño, finely chopped
1 cup (250 mL) corn kernels (page 252)
¼ cup (50 mL) chopped fresh cilantro
10 6-inch (15 cm) flour tortillas

1. In a bowl, combine mayonnaise, cheese, chipotles, corn and cilantro. Mixture should just hold together.
2. Arrange tortillas on work surface in a single layer. Spoon mixture over half of each tortilla (don't overfill). Fold other half over filling and press together firmly.
3. Grill quesadillas for about 1 to 2 minutes per side, or until cheese melts and tortillas are marked with grill marks. Cut each tortilla into thirds.

MAKES 30 PIECES

Curried Lentil Samosas

This is my version of a delicious recipe from Julianne Curran, manager of market inno-vation for Pulse Canada (pulses are the edible seeds of legumes like lentils, beans, peas and chickpeas). You can also make bigger triangles or mini strudels (page 225) and serve these as a main course. If you use olive oil to brush the pastry, the dish is also vegan.

 1 tbsp (15 mL) extra-virgin olive oil
 1 small onion, finely chopped
 1 tbsp (15 mL) curry paste
 1 tsp (5 mL) kosher salt
 Pinch cayenne or aleppo pepper
 1 small sweet potato, peeled, cut in ¼-inch (5 mm) dice and cooked
 1 cup (250 mL) cooked green lentils (preferably du Puy lentils)
 1 tbsp (15 mL) currants
 1 tbsp (15 mL) lemon juice
 2 tsp (10 mL) honey
 10 sheets phyllo pastry
 ⅓ cup (75 mL) melted butter or extra-virgin olive oil
 ½ cup (125 mL) panko or dry breadcrumbs

1. Heat oil in a large, deep skillet over medium heat. Add onion and cook for a few minutes, or until translucent

2. Add curry paste, salt and cayenne. Cook for a few minutes.

3. Stir in well-drained sweet potato, lentils, currants, lemon juice and honey. Cool.

4. Lay out one sheet of phyllo while keeping the rest covered so it doesn't dry out. Lightly brush phyllo sheet with melted butter and sprinkle with breadcrumbs. Cut sheet crosswise into 3 strips about 4 inches (10 cm) wide.

5. Spoon 1 tbsp (15 mL) filling on piece of phyllo about 1 inch (2.5 cm) from bottom on right side. Fold left half of phyllo over right (like a book) to cover filling. Brush phyllo with butter and sprinkle with breadcrumbs. Fold up on the diagonal (like a flag) to form a triangle. Brush lightly with butter. Repeat with remaining phyllo and filling.

6. Place pastries in a single layer on a parchment-lined baking sheet. Bake in a preheated 375°F (190°C) oven for 20 minutes, or until golden. (You can freeze them baked or unbaked. Cook from the frozen state for about 25 minutes.)

MAKES 30 TRIANGLES

Vegetarian Lasagna Casserole

This is my very favorite lasagna, and it works for everyone. For lactose-intolerant eaters, use Lappi instead of the fontina, and omit the Parmesan.

If you make this ahead, reheat it at 350°F (180°C) for 45 minutes, or until bubbling. The lasagna also freezes well (I cut it into serving portions and freeze them individually).

2 tbsp (25 mL) extra-virgin olive oil

1 onion, chopped

3 cloves garlic, finely chopped

Pinch hot red pepper flakes

8 oz (250 g) cremini (brown button) mushrooms, chopped

8 oz (250 g) Asian eggplants, chopped

8 oz (250 g) zucchini, chopped

8 oz (250 g) carrots, peeled and chopped

8 oz (250 g) butternut squash, peeled and chopped

1 28-oz (796 mL) can plum tomatoes, with juices

2 tsp (10 mL) kosher salt

¼ tsp (1 mL) pepper

3 tbsp (45 mL) butter

¼ cup (50 mL) all-purpose flour

3 cups (750 mL) milk, hot

½ tsp (2 mL) hot red pepper sauce

2 cups (500 mL) grated fontina cheese, divided

Salt and pepper to taste

¾ lb (375 g) curly or flat egg noodles

½ cup (125 mL) grated Parmesan cheese, optional

1. Heat oil in a large, deep skillet over medium heat. Add onion, garlic and hot pepper flakes. Cook gently for 5 to 8 minutes, or until softened.

2. Add mushrooms, eggplants, zucchini, carrots and squash. Cook for 15 to 20 minutes, or until lightly browned and any liquid in pan has evaporated.

3. Add tomatoes, salt and pepper and bring to a boil. Cook for 20 minutes, breaking up tomatoes, until sauce is reduced and thick. Taste and adjust seasonings if necessary.

4. Meanwhile, melt butter in a large saucepan over medium heat. Whisk in flour and cook gently for 2 minutes, but do not brown. Whisk in hot milk and bring to a boil.

5. Add hot pepper sauce and cook, stirring often, for 10 minutes. Add 1 cup (250 mL) grated cheese. Season with salt and pepper.

6. Bring a large pot of salted water to a boil. Add noodles, return to a boil and cook for 5 to 8 minutes, or until tender. Drain well.

7. To assemble, smear about ½ cup (125 mL) cheese sauce over bottom of a buttered 13- x 9-inch (3 L) baking dish. Spread noodles in dish. Spoon vegetables over noodles. Spoon remaining cheese sauce over vegetables. Sprinkle with remaining 1 cup (250 mL) cheese and Parmesan, if using.

8. Place baking dish on a foil-lined baking sheet. Bake, uncovered, in a preheated 350°F (180°C) oven for 40 to 45 minutes, or until hot and lightly browned.

MAKES 8 TO 10 SERVINGS

New Wave Caesar Salad

Caesar salad has been popular for so many years, and it has evolved with the times. Originally recipes called for raw eggs, but now I use mayonnaise as a base. Roasted garlic makes the dressing rich and delicious. I also like to add crunchy pecans and smoky grilled corn—a tip from Hugh Carpenter. My son, Mark, has always loved Caesar salad. But when he became lactose intolerant, I began to use Lappi instead of Parmesan.

DRESSING
⅓ cup (75 mL) mayonnaise
2 tbsp (25 mL) lemon juice
2 cloves garlic, minced, or 1 head roasted garlic
1½ tbsp (22 mL) brown sugar
½ cup (125 mL) extra-virgin olive oil

SALAD
2 heads Romaine lettuce, broken in pieces or leaves left whole
2 cups (500 mL) croutons
1½ cups (375 mL) corn kernels, grilled (page 252) or raw, optional
2 cups (500 mL) cherry tomatoes, optional
1 cup (250 mL) toasted pecans, optional
2 oz (60 g) Parmesan cheese, shaved, optional

1. To prepare dressing, in a bowl, combine mayonnaise, lemon juice, garlic, sugar and oil.
2. To prepare salad, arrange lettuce in a shallow serving dish. Top with croutons, corn, cherry tomatoes, nuts and cheese, if using.
3. Drizzle salad with dressing and toss well.

MAKES 8 TO 10 SERVINGS

Croutons

Cut a baguette into ½-inch (1 cm) chunks and place in a large bowl. Toss with ¼ cup (50 mL) extra-virgin olive oil, 1 tsp (5 mL) kosher salt, a pinch hot red pepper flakes, cayenne or aleppo pepper and 2 minced cloves garlic.

Spread croutons on a baking sheet. Bake in a preheated 350°F (180°C) oven for 10 to 15 minutes, or until crusty on the outside but still a little chewy inside. Freeze what you don't use.

Lemon Tiramisu

I make lots of versions of tiramisu, but I have to say that this one is pretty irresistible. Everyone loves it, and it even freezes well. Make it a day before serving and refrigerate it, or make it up to two months ahead and freeze.

In this recipe the egg whites remain uncooked, so if you don't want to use regular eggs, buy pasteurized egg whites. You can make it in a shallow baking dish and serve it in squares, make it in a trifle dish and serve it in scoops or make it in individual wine glasses. If you want to serve small portions, serve it in shooter glasses—adorable! Serve plain or with Mixed Berry Salad (page 233). To make a passionfruit tiramisu, use passionfruit curd instead of the lemon curd.

1 ½ cups (375 mL) lemon curd
1 lb (500 g) mascarpone cheese
¾ cup (175 mL) granulated sugar
¾ cup (175 mL) water
6 pasteurized egg whites (about ¾ cup / 175 mL)

LADYFINGERS
½ cup (125 mL) lemon juice
½ cup (125 mL) granulated sugar
½ cup (125 mL) limoncello (lemon liqueur)
¼ cup (50 mL) vodka
12 oz (375 g) dry Italian ladyfingers (e.g., Savoidardi), approx.
8 oz (250 g) white chocolate, shaved

1. In a bowl, combine lemon curd and mascarpone.
2. In a small saucepan, combine sugar and water and bring to a boil. Cook for 5 to 6 minutes, or until syrup forms a soft ball when dropped into a cup of cold water.
3. In a large bowl, beat egg whites with an electric mixer until stiff peaks form. Continue to beat while slowly adding sugar syrup. Beat on high speed for 5 to 10 minutes, or until cool.
4. Stir one-quarter of beaten whites into mascarpone mixture and then fold in remaining whites.
5. To prepare ladyfingers, in a small saucepan, combine lemon juice and sugar and bring to a boil. Cook for 2 minutes. Add limoncello and vodka and transfer to a shallow dish.
6. To assemble, quickly dip a few ladyfingers at a time into lemon syrup (do not let them get soggy). Place in a single layer in a 13- x 9-inch (3 L) baking dish. Spread with a layer of mascarpone mixture. Repeat layers, ending with mascarpone. Do not worry if you do not use all the ladyfingers or dipping mixture or if you need a little more.
7. Sprinkle dessert with white chocolate, cover and refrigerate for at least 6 hours before serving.

MAKES 10 TO 12 SERVINGS

Lemon Curd

In a saucepan, combine 1 cup (250 mL) granulated sugar, ¾ cup (175 mL) lemon juice, 1 tsp (5 mL) grated lemon peel and ¼ cup (50 mL) butter. Bring to a boil.

In a bowl, beat 6 egg yolks and 2 whole eggs. Beat sugar mixture into eggs and then return to saucepan. Continue to cook over medium heat for 2 to 3 minutes, or until mixture comes to a boil and thickens slightly. Strain into a bowl and chill.

Makes about 1½ cups (375 mL).

Passionfruit Curd

Use ½ cup (125 mL) passionfruit puree and ¼ cup (50 mL) lemon juice instead of ¾ cup (175 mL) lemon juice. Omit grated lemon peel.

BRUSCHETTA WITH GREEN OLIVES AND HERBS
RISOTTO WITH CORN AND MUSHROOMS
OR
SPAGHETTI WITH ROASTED CHERRY TOMATO SAUCE
ITALIAN SALAD
LEMON PUDDING CAKE

fast food italian

SERVES 6

Y ou can never have too many last-minute menus. Here's a simple and completely manageable meal that you can put together after work, even if your guests walk in the door with you. Whip up the simple but delicious pasta dish, or turn dinner preparation into a kitchen party and put your guests to work making the risotto.

Assemble the dessert first, and it can bake in the oven while you are eating the main course (if you have time, you can also make it ahead).

Bruschetta with Green Olives and Herbs

Bruschetta has become so popular that there are now entire restaurants in Italy and North America dedicated to serving grilled or toasted bread topped with everything from tomato salsas and cheese to smoked fish pâtés.

This topping is also delicious on steaks, chops or grilled tuna. It keeps for a few weeks in the refrigerator, so it is easy to have on hand. Use black olives instead of green if you prefer.

1 clove garlic, peeled
2 tbsp (25 mL) coarsely chopped fresh parsley
3 large fresh sage leaves
1 tbsp (15 mL) fresh thyme
1 cup (250 mL) pitted green olives
2 tbsp (25 mL) extra-virgin olive oil, approx.

GRILLED BREAD
20 slices baguette
¼ cup (50 mL) extra-virgin olive oil
½ tsp (2 mL) kosher salt

1. In a food processor, chop garlic, parsley, sage and thyme.
2. Add olives and chop until mixture forms a paste. Add oil if necessary. Taste and adjust seasonings.
3. Brush bread very lightly with oil and sprinkle with salt. Grill in a sandwich press or grill pan or on barbecue, or place in a single layer on a baking sheet and toast in a preheated 350°F (180°C) oven for 10 minutes.
4. Spread a little olive paste on each piece of bread.

MAKES 20 PIECES

Risotto with Corn and Mushrooms

This is a very quick dish to put together at the last minute, especially if you let your guests help you chop and stir. Start cooking the onions and rice and then cook the mushrooms and corn in a separate pan at the same time. (If you have time, you can cook the corn and mushrooms ahead, but the rice should be cooked just before serving.) Stir the cooked vegetables into the rice at the end, add butter and cheese if you wish and then serve it immediately (risotto should be eaten as soon as it is cooked).

Make risotto cakes with any leftovers.

6 to 7 cups (1.5 to 1.75 L) vegetable stock or chicken stock
¼ cup (50 mL) extra-virgin olive oil, divided
1 onion, finely chopped
2 cloves garlic, finely chopped
2 cups (500 mL) short-grain Italian rice
1 shallot, sliced
1 lb (500 g) cremini (brown button) mushrooms, sliced
2 cups (500 mL) corn kernels
2 tbsp (25 mL) butter, optional
½ cup (125 mL) grated Parmesan cheese, optional
Salt and pepper to taste
¼ cup (50 mL) coarsely chopped fresh parsley

1. Bring stock to a boil in a saucepan. Reduce heat to low and keep hot. (If you are using unsalted stock, add 1 tsp/15 mL kosher salt.)
2. Heat 2 tbsp (25 mL) oil in a large, deep skillet over medium heat. Add onion and garlic and cook gently for 3 to 4 minutes, or until fragrant but not brown.
3. Add rice and cook, stirring, for 2 minutes.
4. Start adding hot stock about ½ cup (125 mL) at a time, stirring, until each addition of liquid has evaporated. Continue to add stock until rice is tender. If rice is not tender after you have used all liquid, start adding boiling water until it is cooked. This should take 18 to 20 minutes in total.
5. Meanwhile, heat remaining 2 tbsp (25 mL) oil in a separate large skillet over medium-high heat (this is where the friends come in; let them stir the risotto while you cook the mushrooms, or vice versa). Add shallot and cook, stirring, for 1 minute. Add mushrooms and cook for 5 to 10 minutes, or until dry. Add corn and cook for 2 minutes.
6. When rice is almost tender, stir in corn and mushrooms. Stir in butter and cheese, if using, and season with salt and pepper. Sprinkle with parsley and serve immediately.

MAKES 6 SERVINGS

Risotto Cakes

Combine 3 to 4 cups (750 mL to 1 L) cooked risotto with 1 beaten egg. Shape into patties about 3 inches (7.5 cm) in diameter and ¾ inch (2 cm) thick.

Heat 2 tbsp (25 mL) butter and 2 tbsp (25 mL) olive oil in a large skillet over medium-high heat. Add risotto cakes and cook for about 5 minutes per side, or until browned and crispy. Serve plain or with tomato sauce (page 144).

Makes 3 to 4 patties.

Spaghetti with Roasted Cherry Tomato Sauce

This is so delicious and easy it is almost unbelievable. Toss in a handful of baby spinach or arugula at the end if you wish.

6 cups (1.5 L) cherry tomatoes (preferably a combination of colors)
¼ cup (50 mL) extra-virgin olive oil
1 tsp (5 mL) kosher salt
¼ tsp (1 mL) pepper
3 cloves garlic, minced
⅓ cup (75 mL) packed fresh basil, roughly torn
1 lb (500 g) spaghetti
Salt and pepper to taste
1 tbsp (15 mL) butter or extra-virgin olive oil

1. In a large bowl, combine tomatoes, oil, salt, pepper, garlic and half the basil. Spread on a parchment-lined baking sheet and roast in a preheated 400°F (200°C) oven for 30 minutes, or until tomatoes start to brown and burst a little.
2. Meanwhile, bring a large pot of salted water to a boil. Add spaghetti and cook for 10 to 12 minutes, or until cooked through but not mushy.
3. Drain pasta well and add hot tomatoes and juices. Season with salt and pepper. Add remaining basil and butter and toss.

MAKES 6 SERVINGS

Italian Salad

When I took cooking classes in Italy with Marcella Hazan, she taught us that Italians do not make a salad dressing as we know it. Instead, they dress their salad.

Here's how. Use about 8 cups (2 L) greens for six people.

You need four people to make an Italian salad: a stingy person with the vinegar (it can be any kind but good balsamic is perfect), a judicious person with the salt, a generous person with the extra-virgin olive oil and a patient person to toss it (most people use too much dressing because they don't toss the salad enough).

Makes 6 servings.

Lemon Pudding Cake

Lemon pudding cake is an old-fashioned dessert that is really delicious. It separates into a pudding and cake. For a casual dinner, make it in a baking dish (spoon it out so the pudding is on top), but for something fancier use ramekins, invert them onto individual plates and drizzle with raspberry sauce.

¼ cup (50 mL) butter
¾ cup (175 mL) granulated sugar, divided
4 eggs, separated
1 tbsp (15 mL) grated lemon peel
⅓ cup (75 mL) all-purpose flour
1¼ cups (300 mL) milk
¼ cup (50 mL) lemon juice

1. In a bowl, beat butter with ½ cup (125 mL) sugar until light. Beat in egg yolks and lemon peel. Whisk in flour until smooth. Whisk in milk and lemon juice.
2. In a large bowl, beat egg whites until light. Gradually add remaining ¼ cup (50 mL) sugar. Continue to beat until egg whites are stiff and glossy. Stir one-quarter of egg whites into lemon mixture and then fold lemon mixture into remaining egg whites.
3. Pour mixture into a buttered 8-inch (2 L) square baking dish or 8 to 10 ramekins that have been sprayed with nonstick cooking spray. Set baking dish or ramekins in a larger pan and fill pan with hot water to come halfway up sides of baking dish. Bake in a preheated 350°F (180°C) oven for 40 to 45 minutes (20 to 25 minutes for ramekins), or until top is lightly browned and feels firm when gently pressed. Cover loosely with foil if top is browning too much. To unmold ramekins, run a knife around edge and immerse bottoms in very hot water. Shake gently before inverting onto serving plates.

MAKES 8 SERVINGS

Raspberry Sauce
Combine 1 cup (250 mL) defrosted raspberry sorbet or pureed fresh or frozen unsweetened raspberries with 1 tbsp (15 mL) icing sugar or sugar syrup (page 86) and 2 tsp (10 mL) raspberry or orange liqueur.

Makes about 1 cup (250 mL).

diner dinner

SERVES 8

No matter how sophisticated our tastes become, we always like food from our childhood. Sometimes we want it the same and sometimes we want it with a twist. Chicken noodle soup with smoked chicken, mini burgers and carrot cake with caramelized frosting are updated diner fare—perfect for a comforting and delicious Friday night dinner.

The soup, the meatloaf or sliders, dessert, mashed vegetables and salad dressing can all be made ahead. Reheat the soup, main course and veg and prepare the salad just before serving.

Smoked Chicken Noodle Soup

Chicken noodle soup is real comfort food, and using smoked chicken adds depth and flavor. Buy a pound of smoked deli chicken or turkey or, best of all, buy a whole smoked chicken.

> 8 cups (2 L) homemade chicken stock (page 36)
> 1 cup (250 mL) baby carrots, cut in half lengthwise
> 2 stalks celery, sliced
> 1 2½-lb (1 kg) smoked chicken, skin and bones discarded, cut in chunks
> 1 cup (250 mL) frozen shelled edamame or green peas
> 2 cups (500 mL) cooked egg noodles
> Salt and pepper to taste
> 1 tbsp (15 mL) chopped fresh dill or parsley, or 2 chopped green onions

1. In a large saucepan, combine stock, carrots and celery. Bring to a boil, reduce heat and cook gently for 5 to 10 minutes, or until carrots are tender.
2. Add chicken, edamame and cooked noodles. Cook for 5 minutes. Season with salt and pepper. Add dill.

MAKES 8 SERVINGS

Chicken Meatloaf with Barbecue Sauce

This is such an easy meatloaf that you will make it all the time. Use your favorite homemade or storebought barbecue sauce (I like Original Bullseye). Serve it plain or with a cherry tomato sauce (page 136), tomato sauce (page 144), or even leftover tomato soup (page 32). Make leftovers into sandwiches or serve over pasta.

This can be made ahead and reheated or served cold. Use all ground chicken or half chicken and half beef. If you don't have time to cook the onions and garlic, use half the amount and add raw to the rest of the ingredients.

2 tbsp (25 mL) extra-virgin olive oil
1 large onion, chopped
2 cloves garlic, finely chopped
2 lb (1 kg) ground chicken
2 eggs, beaten
½ cup (125 mL) barbecue sauce
2 tsp (10 mL) kosher salt
1 tsp (5 mL) ground cumin
2 tbsp (25 mL) chopped fresh parsley
1 cup (250 mL) panko or fresh breadcrumbs

TOPPING
2 tbsp (25 mL) barbecue sauce

1. Heat oil in a large skillet over medium heat. Add onion and garlic and cook gently for 15 minutes, or until soft and tender but not brown. Cool.
2. In a large bowl, combine chicken, eggs, barbecue sauce, salt, cumin, parsley, bread-crumbs and onion mixture. Knead together lightly.
3. Place chicken mixture in a 9- x 5-inch (2 L) loaf pan. Cover with parchment paper. Bake in a preheated 350°F (180°C) oven for 1 hour.
4. Uncover, smear with barbecue sauce and bake for 30 minutes longer. Let rest for 10 to 15 minutes before slicing.

MAKES 8 SERVINGS

Meatball Sliders

When Anna came back from New York, she reported that meatball sliders and mini burgers were all the rage. (That's what happens when your kids grow up—they go to New York instead of you!) Now mini burgers and sliders are everywhere. Use dinner rolls for the buns, or you can even use gougères (page 258) or make small buns yourself using challah dough (page 94–95). Count on two per person. (The cooked meatballs also freeze well.)

Use all chicken or all beef instead of a combination. Serve as an appetizer or main course. You can also eat the meatballs on their own or serve them over pasta. In the summer I grill the mini burgers and serve them in buns with guacamole (page 152).

TOMATO SAUCE

2 tbsp (25 mL) extra-virgin olive oil

1 onion, chopped

3 cloves garlic, finely chopped

Pinch hot red pepper flakes

1 28-oz (796 mL) can plum tomatoes, with juices, chopped

1 tsp (5 mL) kosher salt

¼ tsp (1 mL) pepper

1 tbsp (15 mL) chopped fresh basil, parsley or oregano

MEATBALLS

1 lb (500 g) ground beef

1 lb (500 g) ground chicken

2 eggs, beaten

1 tbsp (15 mL) Worcestershire sauce

1 cup (250 mL) panko or fresh breadcrumbs

2 tbsp (25 mL) chopped fresh parsley

2 tsp (10 mL) kosher salt

¼ tsp (1 mL) pepper

2 tbsp (25 mL) extra-virgin olive oil

20 dinner rolls

1. Heat oil in a large saucepan over medium heat. Add onion, garlic and hot pepper flakes and cook gently for 3 to 5 minutes, or until tender.

2. Add tomatoes and bring to a boil. Reduce heat and simmer gently for 10 minutes, or until thickened.

3. Add salt, pepper and basil. Puree sauce. Taste and adjust seasonings if necessary.

4. Meanwhile, to prepare meatballs, in a large bowl, combine beef and chicken. Mix in eggs, Worcestershire, breadcrumbs, parsley, salt and pepper. Form mixture into balls, using about 3 tbsp (45 mL) for each. Flatten slightly.

5. Heat oil in a large skillet over medium-high heat. Add meatballs in batches and cook for a few minutes on each side, or until brown.

6. Add meatballs to sauce, cover and cook for 10 to 15 minutes, or until cooked through. Add ½ cup (125 mL) water if sauce seems dry.

7. Cut rolls in half. Place a meatball and a little sauce in each bun.

MAKES 20 SLIDERS

Potato and Carrot Mash

Today you can buy all kinds of exotic fresh vegetables year round, but when I was a kid potatoes and carrots were the most commonly available. They're still a great combination.

   1 lb (500 g) Yukon Gold potatoes, peeled and cut in chunks
   1 lb (500 g) sweet potatoes, peeled and cut in chunks
   1 lb (500 g) carrots, thinly sliced
   ¼ cup (50 mL) extra-virgin olive oil
   Salt and pepper to taste

1. Place potatoes, sweet potatoes and carrots in a large pot of salted water and bring to a boil. Reduce heat and cook gently for 20 to 35 minutes, or until very tender.
2. Drain well (reserve a little cooking liquid in case you need it) and mash with a potato masher. Mash in oil, salt and pepper. If mixture is too thick, add a little hot cooking liquid.

   MAKES 8 SERVINGS

Iceberg Lettuce Wedges with Thousand Island Dressing

Some chefs think iceberg lettuce is tasteless and old-fashioned, but in fact it is crisp, refreshing and sweet, and it is used a lot in Mexican, Southwestern and Asian recipes. Of course you could also substitute Boston lettuce (if you are determined to be a lettuce snob!).

This dressing has stood the test of time and is perfect in wraps, club sandwiches or burgers.

It is tricky to wash the lettuce and keep it in chunks. An old chef's trick is to hit the lettuce core side down on the counter until it loosens. Pull out the core (like a plug!) and then rinse the lettuce, discarding any bruised leaves.

You can also serve this as an appetizer.

1 cup (250 mL) mayonnaise
¼ cup (50 mL) chili sauce (e.g., Heinz) or ketchup
1 sweet pickle, finely chopped, or 2 tbsp (25 mL) green relish
1 tbsp (15 mL) granulated sugar
1 tbsp (15 mL) white vinegar, cider vinegar or rice vinegar
2 tsp (10 mL) paprika (preferably smoked)
2 heads iceberg lettuce (about 1 lb/ 500 g each)

1. In a bowl, whisk together mayonnaise, chili sauce, pickle, sugar, vinegar and paprika. Taste and adjust seasonings if necessary.
2. Cut each head of lettuce into 8 wedges and serve two wedges per person.
3. Drizzle lettuce with dressing. Dust top with a little extra paprika if you wish.

MAKES 8 SERVINGS

Carrot Tube Cake

This cake is delicious on its own and out of this world with the caramel cream cheese frosting (adapted from Mitchell Davis's cookbook *Kitchen Sense*). Or you can use a regular cream cheese icing or drizzle the cake with a dairy-free lemon glaze.

You can also bake cupcakes and pipe the icing on top in a big teardrop.

4 eggs
¾ cup (175 mL) granulated sugar
¾ cup (175 mL) brown sugar
¾ cup (175 mL) vegetable oil
2 cups (500 mL) all-purpose flour
2 tsp (10 mL) baking powder
½ tsp (2 mL) baking soda
1 tsp (5 mL) ground cinnamon
¼ tsp (1 mL) ground nutmeg
¼ tsp (1 mL) kosher salt
2 cups (500 mL) finely grated carrots, packed
¾ cup (175 mL) drained crushed pineapple
¾ cup (175 mL) chopped toasted walnuts
¾ cup (175 mL) raisins

CARAMEL CREAM CHEESE FROSTING (OPTIONAL)
¾ cup (175 mL) granulated sugar
3 tbsp (45 mL) water
½ cup (125 mL) whipping cream
8 oz (250 g) cream cheese, cut in small pieces
½ cup (125 mL) butter, cut in small pieces
2 tsp (10 mL) vanilla paste or pure vanilla extract

1. In a large bowl, beat eggs, granulated sugar and brown sugar until light. Beat in oil.

2. In a separate bowl, combine flour, baking powder, baking soda, cinnamon, nutmeg and salt. Stir flour mixture into egg mixture just until combined. Stir in carrots, pineapple, walnuts and raisins.

3. Spoon batter into a 10-inch (25 cm) tube pan that has been oiled or sprayed with nonstick cooking spray. Bake in a preheated 350°F (180°C) oven for 1 to 1¼ hours, or until a cake tester comes out clean. (You can also bake batter in 18 muffin cups or 36 mini cups for 20 to 25 minutes.) Cool for 10 minutes. Remove from pan. Cool completely before icing.

4. If you are making frosting, stir sugar and water in a large saucepan over medium-high heat until sugar dissolves. Bring to a boil and stop stirring. Brush any sugar crystals down sides of pan with a pastry brush dipped in cold water. Cook for 6 to 8 minutes, without stirring, or until caramel turns a deep golden brown. Remove from heat.

5. Standing back, add whipping cream. Stir to dissolve. Return to a gentle heat and stir until smooth. Cool completely.

6. In a large bowl, beat cream cheese and butter until smooth. Beat in vanilla and caramel. Chill frosting over a bowl of ice and water until spreadable, or freeze, stirring every 10 minutes, for 30 minutes, or until frosting holds its shape well (don't worry, it will eventually set). Ice cake with frosting. (I often ice just the top and then drizzle the cake with a little reserved caramel.)

MAKES 10 SERVINGS

Lemon Glaze

Combine 1 cup (250 mL) sifted icing sugar and 2 tbsp (25 mL) lemon juice.

Makes about 1 cup (250 mL).

Best Ever Cream Cheese Icing

Combine 12 oz (375 g) diced cream cheese and ¾ cup (175 mL) diced butter until smooth. Beat in 3 cups (750 mL) sifted icing sugar and 2 tsp (10 mL) vanilla paste or pure vanilla extract.

Makes about 2½ cups (625 mL).

CLASSIC GUACAMOLE

HANGER STEAK WITH WORCESTERSHIRE MARINADE

ROASTED FENNEL

SAUTÉED KING MUSHROOMS

ROASTED BABY POTATOES WITH SHALLOTS AND MUSTARD

APPLE PUFF PANCAKE

fast food family

SERVES 6

I am a fast cook, but even for me some recipes are faster than others, so when Friday night comes too quickly after a hard work week, I turn to recipes that are quick and easy but taste as if you have been cooking for days.

This entire menu can be put together after you get home from work. I usually marinate the steak and make the guacamole first. The dessert can bake while you are eating the main course.

Classic Guacamole

The trick to making great guacamole is ripe avocados. It can be hard to find them ripe the day you need them, so I like to keep a few on hand. I ripen them on the counter and then put them in the refrigerator, where they will usually keep for a week. If you are in a hurry, put them in a bag or canister of uncooked rice, and they will ripen more quickly. (Don't bother trying to make guacamole with an unripe avocado.)

Everyone has a favorite guacamole recipe. Does it have garlic? Tomatoes? Jalapeños? Lime juice? The only thing it always has is avocados. Use this recipe as a base for your own version.

Serve this as a dip with tortilla chips or flour or corn tortillas. Or use it as a topping on burgers, steaks, fish, burritos, soups or salads.

1 small jalapeño, seeded and finely chopped
⅓ cup (75 mL) chopped fresh cilantro
1 tsp (5 mL) kosher salt
2 tbsp (25 mL) lime juice, approx.
1 clove garlic, minced, optional
2 ripe avocados (about 8 oz/250 g each)

1. In a bowl, combine jalapeño, cilantro, salt, lime juice and garlic, if using.
2. Just before serving, cut avocados in half. Remove pits. Scoop out flesh and dice. Add to mixture in bowl and mash with a potato masher. It can be as smooth or chunky as you wish. Taste and adjust seasonings. If not serving immediately, cover surface of guacamole directly with plastic wrap to help prevent discoloration. (Lots of lime juice also does the trick.)

MAKES ABOUT 1½ CUPS (375 ML)

Hanger Steak with Worcestershire Marinade

I discovered hanger steak when I went to Las Vegas to speak at a conference. I didn't like Las Vegas that much, but I loved the hanger steak at L'Atelier, Joel Robuchon's "downscale" restaurant. (When I was there, there were two Joel Robuchon restaurants in Las Vegas. One was expensive—the one I went to—and the other was *really* expensive.)

Hanger steak is a favorite of butchers. Traditionally it's the cut they got to take home because it was considered too ordinary for customers. But like flank steak, flat-iron steak, skirt steak and tri-tip, it is really tender and delicious if cooked rare and thinly sliced, and it is becoming very popular.

This marinade is my version of one from Cumbrae Butchers in Toronto. Be sure to ask your butcher to split the steak and remove the "seam." (You will have two pieces from a hanger steak—one larger and one smaller.) If you can't find hanger steak, use flank steak, or even a sirloin will work brilliantly.

1 tbsp (15 mL) paprika
1 tsp (5 mL) kosher salt
1 tsp (5 mL) pepper
3 cloves garlic, minced
¼ cup (50 mL) Worcestershire sauce
¼ cup (50 mL) extra-virgin olive oil
2 lb (500 g) hanger steak

1. In a small bowl, combine paprika, salt, pepper, garlic, Worcestershire and oil. Rub into steak. Marinate in refrigerator until ready to cook.
2. Grill thicker part of steak for about 5 minutes per side and thinner part for 3 minutes per side, or until a meat thermometer registers 125 to 130°F (52 to 54°C) for medium-rare. You can also sear the steak in a lightly oiled hot, heavy pan for 1 to 2 minutes per side. Finish cooking in a 425°F (220°C) oven for 7 to 10 minutes, or until medium-rare.
3. Let steak rest for a few minutes before carving thinly on the diagonal.

MAKES 6 SERVINGS

Roasted Fennel

When fennel is raw, it tastes a lot like licorice, but it is very gentle when cooked. It is also delicious grilled.

2 bulbs fennel
2 tbsp (25 mL) extra-virgin olive oil
2 tbsp (25 mL) fresh thyme, or ½ tsp (2 mL) dried
1 tsp (5 mL) kosher salt
¼ tsp (1 mL) pepper

1. Trim fronds and bottom from fennel and cut each bulb into 6 wedges through stem (so wedges will hold together). Sprinkle with oil, thyme, salt and pepper.
2. Arrange wedges on a parchment-lined baking sheet and bake in a preheated 425°F (220°C) oven for 25 to 30 minutes, or until tender.

MAKES 6 SERVINGS

Sautéed King Mushrooms

King mushrooms are meaty and delicious. They are less watery than other mushrooms, so they don't shrink as much and cook quickly (they can also be barbecued). They are becoming more available (look for them in Chinese grocery stores), but if you can't find them, use portobellos.

This is a beautiful side dish to serve with steak, veal chops or roast chicken.

3 tbsp (45 mL) extra-virgin olive oil
¾ lb (375 g) king mushrooms, cut in slices about ¼ inch (5 mm) thick
½ tsp (2 mL) truffle salt or sea salt (e.g., Maldon)
2 tsp (10 mL) aged balsamic vinegar

1. Heat oil in a large skillet over medium-high heat. Add mushrooms in a single layer (you will have to do this in batches) and cook for 2 to 3 minutes per side, or until nicely browned.
2. Arrange mushrooms on a serving platter. Sprinkle with salt and drizzle with balsamic.

MAKES 6 SERVINGS

Roasted Baby Potatoes with Shallots and Mustard

When you are using baby potatoes, buy the cleanest ones you can find—Yukon Gold, red, fingerlings—to save on scrubbing time!

3 tbsp (45 mL) extra-virgin olive oil
1 tbsp (15 mL) grainy mustard
1 tsp (5 mL) kosher salt
½ tsp (2 mL) pepper
1 clove garlic, minced
1 tbsp (15 mL) chopped fresh rosemary, or ½ tsp (2 mL) dried
2 lb (1 kg) baby Yukon Gold or other small potatoes, cut in half or in quarters
2 shallots, thinly sliced
2 tbsp (25 mL) chopped fresh parsley

1. In a large bowl, combine oil, mustard, salt, pepper, garlic and rosemary. Add potatoes and shallots and toss together.
2. Spread potatoes and shallots on a parchment-lined baking sheet. Bake in a preheated 425°F (220°C) oven for 45 to 60 minutes, or until lightly browned and tender.
3. Sprinkle with parsley before serving.

MAKES 6 SERVINGS

Apple Puff Pancake

When I have nothing planned for dessert, my family says, "Just make that apple pancake thing." And it's true—this amazing dessert can be ready for the oven in no time, and it only takes 20 minutes to bake.

Use firm apples such as Fuji, Spy or Golden Delicious.

¼ cup (50 mL) butter or vegetable oil
2 apples, peeled and sliced
½ tsp (2 mL) ground cinnamon
3 tbsp (45 mL) brown sugar
3 eggs
1 tbsp (15 mL) granulated sugar
½ cup (125 mL) milk or soy milk
½ cup (125 mL) all-purpose flour
2 tbsp (25 mL) icing sugar, sifted

1. Heat butter in a 9- or 10-inch (23 or 25 cm) heavy nonstick ovenproof skillet over medium-high heat. Transfer 2 tbsp (25 mL) melted butter to a food processor or blender, leaving remaining butter in skillet. it is also great for brunch.
2. Add apples, cinnamon and brown sugar to skillet and cook for 10 minutes, or until apples are tender.
3. Meanwhile, add eggs, granulated sugar, milk and flour to food processor. Blend until smooth. Pour over apples in hot skillet.
4. Bake in a preheated 425°F (220°C) oven for 20 to 25 minutes, or until browned and puffed.
5. Shake pan to loosen pancake. Invert onto a serving platter and dust with icing sugar.

MAKES 6 SERVINGS

FISH CAKES WITH CILANTRO MINT CHUTNEY

TAMARIND AND COCONUT-GLAZED CHICKEN THIGHS

CUMIN-FLAVORED BASMATI RICE

WHEAT BERRY, LENTIL AND CHICKPEA SALAD

CARROTS AND GREEN BEANS WITH ONIONS AND MUSTARD SEEDS

GRILLED PINEAPPLE WITH CHAI SPICES

indian dinner

SERVES 6

I love Indian food. The flavors are so complex and exciting. And I have been lucky to have learned about Indian cooking from the very best—first and foremost actress and award-winning authority on Indian cooking Madhur Jaffrey; Meena Patak, the force behind Patak's Indian foods; and Vikram Vij, owner of Vancouver's fabulous Indian restaurant—all of whom have taught at my school. The flavors in this menu are inspired by these amazing cooks.

   The chutney, dessert and salad can all be made ahead, the fish cakes can be cooked ahead and reheated, and the chicken can be marinated ahead of time. Make the basmati rice (or just plain steamed rice) ahead and keep warm.

Fish Cakes with Cilantro Mint Chutney

No trip to Vancouver would be complete without a visit to Vij's modern Indian restaurant. I first ate there ten years ago, and since then Vikram has taught at my school a few times, introducing his wonderful flavors to my students and staff.

These delicious fish cakes were inspired by him. They are a great way to use up left-over fish, and you can even use canned. Serve them as appetizers or as a main course. They are also delicious at room temperature.

1 lb (500 g) cooked fish (salmon, cod, halibut, etc.),
   flaked (about 2 cups / 500 mL)
1 lb (500 g) potatoes, peeled, cooked and mashed (about 1 ½ cups / 375 mL)
4 oz (125 g) sweet potatoes, peeled, cooked and mashed (about ½ cup / 125 mL)
2 tbsp (25 mL) all-purpose flour
3 green onions, finely chopped
1 large jalapeño, seeded and chopped
1 egg, beaten
⅓ cup (75 mL) chopped fresh cilantro
1 tbsp (15 mL) garam masala or ground cumin
2 tsp (10 mL) ground coriander
2 tsp (10 mL) kosher salt
¼ cup (50 mL) vegetable oil

CILANTRO MINT CHUTNEY
1 jalapeño, seeded and cut in chunks
½ cup (125 mL) fresh cilantro
½ cup (125 mL) fresh mint
½ tsp (2 mL) kosher salt
2 tbsp (25 mL) granulated sugar
2 tbsp (25 mL) lime juice

1. In a large bowl, combine fish, potatoes, sweet potatoes, flour, green onions, jalapeño, egg, cilantro, garam masala, coriander and salt. Shape into 24 patties.
2. Heat oil in one or two large skillets over medium-high heat. Cook fish cakes for 3 minutes per side, or until crispy and hot.
3. To make chutney, in a food processor, combine jalapeño, cilantro, mint, salt, sugar and lime juice. Add a little water if necessary to thin.
4. Serve fish cakes with chutney.

MAKES 24 SMALL CAKES

Tamarind and Coconut-glazed Chicken Thighs

This recipe is a real winner. My kids loved it even when they were really fussy eaters. Chicken thighs are so juicy and moist that they don't dry out easily on the grill.

¾ cup (175 mL) coconut milk or unflavored yogurt
2 tbsp (25 mL) tamarind paste
3 cloves garlic, minced
1 tbsp (15 mL) kosher salt
1 tbsp (15 mL) garam masala or ground cumin
1 tsp (5 mL) cayenne
12 boneless chicken thighs (with skin or skinless)
1 lemon, cut in wedges
Sprigs of fresh cilantro

1. In a large bowl, combine coconut milk, tamarind paste, garlic, salt, garam masala and cayenne. Add chicken and turn to coat well with marinade. Cover and refrigerate for 4 to 8 hours.
2. Grill chicken for 8 to 10 minutes per side. (You could also brown the chicken in a skillet on the stove, place on a parchment-lined baking sheet and finish cooking in a 375°F/190°C oven for 20 to 30 minutes, or until thoroughly cooked.)
3. Garnish with lemon wedges and cilantro.

MAKES 6 SERVINGS

Cumin-flavored Basmati Rice

Basmati rice has a fragrance and flavor all its own, but the cumin in this recipe makes it a little more aromatic.

> 1½ cups (375 mL) basmati rice
> 2 tbsp (25 mL) vegetable oil
> 1 onion, chopped
> 1 carrot, grated
> 1 tbsp (15 mL) cumin seeds
> 2½ cups (625 mL) water
> ½ tsp (2 mL) kosher salt, or more to taste

1. Rinse rice in several changes of cold water until water runs clear.
2. Heat oil in a saucepan over medium-high heat. Add onion, carrot and cumin seeds and cook for 5 to 10 minutes, or until onions just start to brown.
3. Add rice and stir to coat with oil. Add water and salt and bring to a boil. Reduce heat, cover and simmer gently for 10 minutes, or until water has been absorbed. Remove from heat and let stand for 10 minutes. Fluff gently before serving.

MAKES 6 SERVINGS

Steamed Jasmine Rice

Rinse 2 cups (500 mL) jasmine or basmati rice well in several changes of water.

Combine rice and 3 cups (750 mL) cold water in a medium saucepan (if you are using brown rice use 3½ cups/875 mL water). Bring to a boil, uncovered. This will take about 5 to 7 minutes. Reduce heat to medium and cook for 5 minutes, or until water has almost been absorbed and potholes appear on surface of rice.

Cover, reduce heat to low and cook for 10 minutes. Turn off heat but leave rice covered for 10 minutes longer. Fluff rice gently before serving.

Makes 6 servings.

Wheat Berry, Lentil and Chickpea Salad

Even people who don't generally like grains seem to love wheat berries—and this salad. Look for wheat berries at health food stores and some supermarkets (if you can't find them, you can always use brown rice).

When I cook wheat berries and lentils, I usually make more than I need and freeze them so I can have them on hand for salads like this.

1 cup (250 mL) frozen green peas, defrosted
1 cup (250 mL) cooked wheat berries
1 cup (250 mL) cooked small green lentils
1 cup (250 mL) cooked or canned chickpeas
3 green onions, chopped
¼ cup (50 mL) chopped fresh mint
1 tbsp (15 mL) chopped fresh cilantro
¼ cup (50 mL) lemon juice
1 tbsp (15 mL) granulated sugar
1 tsp (5 mL) kosher salt
1 tsp (5 mL) pepper

1. In a large bowl, combine peas, wheat berries, lentils, chickpeas, green onions, mint and cilantro.
2. In a small bowl, combine lemon juice, sugar, salt and pepper.
3. Add dressing to salad and toss.

MAKES 6 SERVINGS

Cooking Wheat Berries

Rinse 1 cup (250 mL) wheat berries and place in a large saucepan. Cover with at least 4 inches (10 cm) cold water. Bring to a boil, reduce heat and simmer gently, covered, for 1 to 1½ hours, or until tender (wheat berries should be slightly chewy but tender). Rinse and drain well.

Makes about 2½ cups (625 mL) cooked wheat berries.

Carrots and Green Beans with
Onions and Mustard Seeds

Vegetables that accompany an Indian meal can be "wet" and saucy or "dry," as in this dish.

> 1 lb (500 g) carrots, cut in diagonal slices ½ inch (1 cm) thick
> 1 lb (500 g) green beans, trimmed and halved
> 1 tbsp (15 mL) vegetable oil
> ½ tsp (2 mL) black mustard seeds
> 1 onion, thinly sliced
> Pinch hot red pepper flakes
> 1 tsp (5 mL) kosher salt

1. Bring a large pot of salted water to a boil. Add carrots and beans and cook for 3 minutes. Drain well.
2. Meanwhile, heat oil in a large skillet over medium-high heat. Add mustard seeds and cook for 30 to 60 seconds, or until they start to pop. (Cover them partially if necessary to keep them from jumping out of the pan.)
3. Add onion and hot pepper flakes and cook for 5 to 10 minutes, or until onion is well browned. Add drained carrots and beans to skillet and turn to coat well. Season with salt.

MAKES 6 SERVINGS

Cooking Green Lentils
Rinse 1 cup (250 mL) lentils and place in a large saucepan. Cover generously with water. Bring to a boil, reduce heat and cook gently for 25 to 35 minutes, or just until tender. Rinse and drain well.

Makes about 2 cups (500 mL) cooked lentils.

Grilled Pineapple with Chai Spices

Chai (which really just means tea) has come to refer to an Indian spiced tea that is very fragrant and flavorful. The mixture of spices can be used in cookies, cakes and for spiced sugar toppings like the one in this recipe.

Pineapple is often sold already peeled and cored. If you can only find a whole pineapple, it is easier to cut it into wedges rather than into rings. Cut the top and bottom off the pineapple, cut it in half lengthwise and then cut each half into 4 wedges. Remove the strip of core and then cut the wedge off the peel.

You can also serve this with a scoop of Coconut Rice Pudding (page 213).

1 pineapple, peeled and cored, cut in 8 rings or wedges
½ cup (125 mL) brown sugar
½ tsp (2 mL) ground cinnamon
¼ tsp (1 mL) ground cardamom
Pinch ground cloves
Pinch ground nutmeg
Pinch ground anise
8 small scoops mango sorbet or vanilla or caramel ice cream
¼ cup (50 mL) sesame crumble, optional

1. Place pineapple slices in a single layer on a baking sheet. Pat very dry.
2. In a small bowl, combine brown sugar, cinnamon, cardamom, cloves, nutmeg and anise. Sprinkle over both sides of pineapple and pat in.
3. Grill pineapple for 2 to 3 minutes per side, or until hot and nicely browned. Serve with sorbet. Sprinkle with sesame crumble, if using.

MAKES 8 SERVINGS

Sesame Crumble

Separate a 1¼-oz (35 g) package of sesame snaps and crumble coarsely. Use as a garnish for salads, soups and desserts.

Makes ¼ cup (50 mL).

standing-up dinner

SERVES 8

Although Friday night dinners are usually served with guests sitting around a table, once in a while, when there aren't enough seats, or there are too many guests, or we're in the middle of house renovations, we serve dinner buffet style and eat standing up (or sitting on the steps, or kneeling beside the coffee table . . .). On those occasions, the food has to be easy to eat.

Most of this menu can be made ahead. Prepare the stew up to the end of Step 3 and refrigerate; reheat it and add the fish just before serving.

Caramelized Onion Mini Quiches

Because tiny quichettes are now available commercially, it is easy to forget how delicious they are when they are homemade. They may seem like a lot of work at first, but after you've made them once or twice, they are pretty easy. They make perfect standing-up food. Just adapt your favorite quiche recipe.

These can be made completely ahead and frozen. (They are so small that they will reheat at 400°F/200°C in 10 to 15 minutes.) Cook lots of onions and freeze some so you can make these more quickly next time.

ALL-PURPOSE PASTRY

2 cups (500 mL) all-purpose flour

½ tsp (2 mL) kosher salt

1 cup (250 mL) butter, cold, cut in pieces

6 tbsp (90 mL) ice water, approx.

FILLING

2 tbsp (25 mL) butter or extra-virgin olive oil

3 large onions, chopped

1 tbsp (15 mL) granulated sugar

2 tbsp (25 mL) balsamic vinegar

3 eggs

1 cup (250 mL) milk or cream

1 tsp (5 mL) kosher salt

½ tsp (2 mL) pepper

½ lb (250 g) Cambozola cheese, crusts removed, diced

2 tbsp (25 mL) chopped fresh tarragon

1. To prepare pastry, in a large bowl, combine flour and salt. Add butter and, using your fingers or a pastry blender, cut in until mixture resembles coarse breadcrumbs. Drizzle with ice water and gather dough into a ball, adding water if necessary. Knead a few times, wrap in plastic wrap and refrigerate for 30 minutes.

2. Roll dough into a large circle about ⅛ inch (3 mm) thick. Using a 3½-inch (9 cm) cookie cutter (or a size to fit your tart pans), cut out as many circles as you can. Press excess dough together lightly, roll out one more time and cut out more circles.

3. Gently press dough into mini tart pans or muffin pans. Line tart shells with cupcake liners and fill with a spoonful of pie weights (try using clean pennies), dried beans or rice. Bake in a preheated 425°F (220°C) oven for 10 minutes. Remove weights and paper.

4. Meanwhile, heat butter in a large skillet over medium-high heat. Add onions and cook for 20 to 25 minutes, or until lightly browned.

5. Add sugar and vinegar and continue to cook for 20 minutes, or until well browned. Cool.

6. In a large bowl, whisk eggs with milk, salt and pepper.

7. Place cooled onions in tart shells. Top with a bit of cheese and tarragon. Spoon in egg mixture. Place tart pans on baking sheets to catch any spills.

8. Bake in a preheated 375°F (190°C) oven for 10 to 15 minutes, or until custard is set and browned on top. Cool for 10 minutes before serving.

MAKES 36 MINI QUICHES

Standing-up Fish Stew

At a buffet dinner Ray and I attended in Australia, we were served a seafood stew in Chinese take-out containers. I make a version now with fish that can be broken apart with a spoon and is easy to eat, either sitting down or standing up. If you want to add shellfish, cut it into bite-sized pieces and add it a few minutes after the fish.

Serve this stew in bowls, or as a sitting-down main course over rice.

¼ cup (50 mL) extra-virgin olive oil
2 onions, diced
1 large carrot, diced
1 stalk celery, diced
2 potatoes, peeled and diced
1 bulb fennel (about ¾ lb / 375 g), trimmed and diced
4 cloves garlic, finely chopped
1 28-oz (796 mL) can plum tomatoes, with juices, pureed
½ cup (125 mL) dry white wine
4 cups (1 L) fish stock, chicken stock or water
1 tbsp (15 mL) fresh thyme, or 1 tsp (5 mL) dried
1 tbsp (15 mL) grated orange peel
2 tsp (10 mL) Worcestershire sauce
¼ tsp (1 mL) hot red pepper flakes
Pinch saffron threads, crushed, optional
1 tbsp (15 mL) kosher salt
½ tsp (2 mL) pepper
2 lb (1 kg) white-fleshed fish fillets (e.g., cod, halibut), cut in large chunks
2 lb (1 kg) salmon fillet (preferably wild), cut in large chunks
2 cups (500 mL) small croutons
½ cup (125 mL) roasted garlic aïoli
2 tbsp (25 mL) chopped fresh parsley

1. Heat oil in a Dutch oven over medium heat. Add onions, carrot, celery, potatoes, fennel and garlic. Cook gently for 5 minutes.
2. Add tomatoes, bring to a boil and cook for 5 minutes.
3. Add wine, stock, thyme, orange peel, Worcestershire sauce, hot pepper flakes and saffron, if using. Season with salt and pepper. Bring to a boil and cook, uncovered, for 10 to 20 minutes, or until slightly thickened.
4. Add fish and cook for 5 to 10 minutes, or just until fish is cooked. Do not stir too much after adding fish or it will break up. Taste and adjust seasonings, if necessary.
5. Serve sprinkled with croutons and aïoli and garnished with parsley.

MAKES 8 TO 10 SERVINGS

Mini Lemon Croutons

In a large bowl, toss 2 cups (500 mL) bread cubes, 2 tbsp (25 mL) extra-virgin olive oil, 1 tsp (5 mL) grated lemon peel and ½ tsp (2 mL) kosher salt. Sauté in a large skillet for 5 minutes, or spread on a baking sheet and bake in a preheated 350°F (180°C) oven for 10 to 15 minutes, or until browned and crisp.

Makes 2 cups (500 mL).

Roasted Garlic

Remove any excess white papery skin from 4 whole heads of garlic. Cut top quarter from each head (the pointed part) to expose tops of cloves. Rub cut surface with a little olive oil.

Wrap garlic heads in foil in a single layer and roast in preheated 375°F (190°C) oven for 40 to 50 minutes, or until garlic is very tender when squeezed.

Cool heads slightly and squeeze out garlic. Refrigerate for up to 2 weeks or freeze (freeze it flat in small resealable freezer bags so you can break off what you need).

Roasted Garlic Aïoli

Squeeze 1 head roasted garlic into ½ cup (125 mL) mayonnaise and puree. Add 1 tbsp (15 mL) lemon juice and ½ tsp (2 mL) hot red pepper sauce.

Makes about ½ cup (125 mL).

Salad Skewers

This is a super-cute salad that is very easy to eat.

16 cherry tomatoes
½ English cucumber, halved, seeded and cut in 1-inch (2.5 cm) chunks
8 oz (250 g) bocconcini cheese, cut in 1-inch (2.5 cm) cubes
16 large pitted black olives
16 large pitted green olives
16 fresh basil leaves

1. Skewer ingredients onto 16 8-inch (20 cm) bamboo skewers.

MAKES 16 SKEWERS

Sesame Bread Biscuits

Quickbreads are just that—a quick way to have irresistible, sensational-smelling home-made bread with dinner.

1 cup (250 mL) all-purpose flour
¾ cup (175 mL) whole wheat flour
2 tbsp (25 mL) granulated sugar
4 tsp (20 mL) baking powder
½ tsp (2 mL) kosher salt
⅓ cup (75 mL) butter, cold, cut in pieces
1 egg, beaten
½ cup (125 mL) milk
1 egg white
2 tbsp (25 mL) sesame seeds
1 tsp (25 mL) coarse salt

1. In a large bowl, combine flours with sugar, baking powder and salt. Add butter and cut in until it is in tiny bits.
2. In a small bowl, combine whole egg and milk. Stir into flour mixture. Gather into a ball and knead gently together.
3. On a floured surface, pat or roll dough into a rectangle about 1 inch (2.5 cm) thick. Cut into 8 squares.
4. In a small bowl, lightly whisk egg white. In a separate small bowl, combine sesame seeds and coarse salt.
5. Brush biscuits lightly with egg white and sprinkle with seeds and salt.
6. Transfer to a double baking sheet (page 26) lined with parchment paper. Bake in a pre-heated 425°F (220°C) for 10 to 12 minutes, or until lightly golden.

MAKES 8 BISCUITS

Sticky Toffee Cake with Butterscotch Sauce

This cake has taken over from tiramisu and chocolate lava cake as today's dessert of choice, and is our favorite at home and at work. Some restaurants make the mistake of calling it sticky date cake, but many people are put off by the idea of dates and won't even try it (when you taste it you'd never guess it contained dates at all). Even chocoholics love this cake, and it doesn't contain chocolate.

I often make individual cakes in muffin pans, and I usually serve it with whipped cream or ice cream as well as the sauce.

This cake was everywhere when I was in Australia, and this recipe is based on a version from Neil Perry, a well-known Sydney restaurateur and chef. It's the best one ever.

12 oz (375 g) pitted dates (about 1½ cups/ 375 mL)
2 cups (500 mL) water
1½ tsp (7 mL) baking soda
⅓ cup (75 mL) butter
1 cup (250 mL) packed brown sugar
3 eggs
1½ cups (375 mL) all-purpose flour
1½ tsp (7 mL) baking powder
½ tsp (2 mL) kosher salt

BUTTERSCOTCH SAUCE
¾ cup (175 mL) packed (preferably dark) brown sugar
1¼ cups (300 mL) whipping cream
½ cup (125 mL) butter, cut in pieces

1. Combine dates and water in a saucepan and bring to a boil. Remove from heat.
2. Add baking soda and let stand for 5 minutes. Puree date mixture.
3. Cream butter and sugar in a bowl with an electric mixer. Beat in eggs one at a time.
4. In a separate bowl, combine flour, baking powder and salt. Gently fold flour mixture into batter alternately with dates, in 3 or 4 additions, beginning and ending with flour.
5. Transfer batter to a buttered and parchment-lined 9-inch (23 cm) round springform pan or 12 to 18 buttered muffin pans. Bake in a preheated 350°F (180°C) oven for about 60 to 75 minutes (20 to 25 minutes for muffins), or until a cake tester comes out clean. Cover with foil if top of cake is getting too dark.
6. Meanwhile, to prepare sauce, in a saucepan, combine sugar, cream and butter. Bring to a boil. Reduce heat and simmer gently for 5 minutes, or until slightly thickened.
7. With a fork or skewer, prick holes in cake when it comes out of oven. Drizzle one third of the sauce over top and allow to sink in. Cool cake for 10 minutes and then invert onto a serving plate. Pour remaining sauce over cake when you serve.

MAKES 8 TO 10 SERVINGS

passover

SERVES 10 TO 12

Passover is an eight-day holiday that celebrates the liberation of the Israelites from Egypt. It begins with one or two nights of Seders—elaborate family dinners at which the story of Passover is told. During Passover it is traditional to eat special foods such as matzah and to avoid yeast and flour. Eastern European Jews also avoid legumes and foods that swell during cooking, such as rice and grains.

In this menu I have tried to blend old favorites with new recipes from here and from Israel. Jewish cooks often have a hard time finding great desserts for Passover, so here are a few of the many delicious ones that I have collected over the years.

These dishes can be used for your Seder meal or any time during Passover (or any other time of year, for that matter). Jews from different backgrounds follow different traditions, so please adjust the recipes to your own needs.

Most of these items can be made ahead, including the desserts, eggplant and salad dressing. The tzimmes and fish cakes can be prepared ahead and reheated; cook the lamb and toss the salad just before serving.

Baba Ghanouj (Smoky Eggplant Dip)

Buy large oval eggplants for this, as they usually have fewer seeds. For a fantastic smoky taste, cook the eggplants over a flame—either on a barbecue or over a medium-high flame on a gas stove. Otherwise bake the eggplants in the oven; the spread will still be delicious.

Serve this with matzah at Passover or with grilled pita or challah at other times. (Sephardic Jews use sesame products during Passover, while Ashkenazi Jews do not. The dip is delicious with or without the tahina.)

2 large eggplants (about 3 lb / 1.5 kg total)

TAHINA MAYONNAISE
2 tbsp (25 mL) lemon juice
2 cloves garlic, minced
1 tsp (5 mL) kosher salt
½ cup (125 mL) mayonnaise
2 tbsp (25 mL) tahina, optional
Dash hot red pepper sauce, optional
2 tbsp (25 mL) chopped fresh cilantro

1. Place eggplants directly on a gas burner or barbecue and turn frequently for 15 to 20 minutes, or until skin is toasted and eggplants are very tender. (Or, place eggplant on a parchment-lined baking sheet and roast in a preheated 400°F/200°C oven for 40 to 50 minutes, or until tender and collapsed.) Cool.
2. Place eggplants in a large sieve set over a bowl and remove and discard skins. Cut eggplants into chunks and press out excess liquid. (If there are big pockets of seeds you can discard them, but do not try to remove all the seeds.)
3. Meanwhile, in a large bowl, whisk together lemon juice, garlic, salt and mayonnaise. Add tahina and hot pepper sauce, if using. Taste and adjust seasonings if necessary. (Do not worry if sauce is thick and unmanageable when you first start mixing; it will smooth out when you add all the ingredients.)
4. Add eggplant and combine well. Sprinkle with cilantro.

MAKES 3 CUPS (750 ML)

Moroccan Fish "Kebabs"

At Passover it is traditional to serve a fish course, and this dish is a wonderful change after years of gefilte (chopped) fish. It is based on something I tasted in a tiny restaurant in the market in Tel Aviv. In Middle Eastern cooking, "kebab" refers to something made with ground meat or fish, not necessarily on a skewer (in North America we would probably call them cakes or patties).

FISH CAKES

2 lb (1 kg) halibut fillets (skin removed), or a combination of halibut and tilapia
    or other white-fleshed fish

1 egg white

¼ cup (50 mL) chopped fresh cilantro or parsley

2 tbsp (25 mL) finely chopped preserved lemon peel (page 69),
    or 1 tbsp (15 mL) grated lemon peel

2 tsp (10 mL) kosher salt

1 tsp (5 mL) ground cumin

1 tsp (5 mL) paprika

¼ tsp (1 mL) cayenne or aleppo pepper

2 tbsp (25 mL) extra-virgin olive oil or vegetable oil

MIDDLE EASTERN TOMATO SAUCE

2 tbsp (25 mL) extra-virgin olive oil

1 onion, chopped

1 clove garlic, chopped

1 tbsp (15 mL) chopped fresh ginger

1 jalapeño, seeded and finely chopped, or hot red pepper sauce to taste

1 tsp (5 mL) ground cumin

¼ tsp (1 mL) ground cinnamon

1 28-oz (796 mL) can plum tomatoes, with juices

1 tbsp (15 mL) honey

Salt and pepper to taste

¼ cup (50 mL) chopped fresh cilantro or parsley

1. To prepare fish cakes, chop fish so that some of it is coarsely chopped and some is finely chopped.
2. In a large bowl, combine fish, egg white, cilantro, preserved lemon, salt, cumin, paprika and cayenne. Form into about 16 small patties about 1½ inches (4 cm) in diameter.
3. Heat oil in a large skillet over medium-high heat. Add fish cakes, in batches, and cook for 2 to 3 minutes per side, or until lightly browned.
4. Meanwhile, to prepare sauce, heat oil in a separate large skillet or saucepan over medium heat. Add onion, garlic, ginger and jalapeño and cook for 2 to 3 minutes, or until tender but not brown.
5. Add cumin and cinnamon and cook for 30 seconds. Add tomatoes, breaking them up with a spoon. Cook for about 10 minutes, or until thickened. Add honey and season with salt and pepper.
6. Add sauce to fish cakes (or vice versa) and cook for about 5 minutes, or until fish is just cooked through. Sprinkle with cilantro.

MAKES 16 PATTIES

Rack of Lamb with Harissa and Charmoula

I usually make a large amount of the harissa and keep it frozen. You can also buy it, but the commercial version is usually very hot, so beware (for this recipe, mix 1 to 2 tsp / 5 to 10 mL storebought harissa with ½ cup / 125 mL olive oil). Charmoula is one of my favorite sauces and can also be used on burgers, grilled chicken and steak.

HARISSA
½ cup (125 mL) extra-virgin olive oil
4 cloves garlic, minced
1 tbsp (15 mL) paprika (preferably smoked)
1 tbsp (15 mL) ground cumin
2 tsp (10 mL) kosher salt
1 tsp (5 mL) cayenne or hot red pepper sauce
4 racks of lamb (chine bone removed)

CHARMOULA DRIZZLE
1 cup (250 mL) mayonnaise
2 cloves garlic, minced
1 tbsp (15 mL) lemon juice
1 tsp (5 mL) hot red pepper sauce
½ tsp (2 mL) ground cumin
1 tbsp (15 mL) paprika (preferably smoked)
2 tbsp (25 mL) finely chopped fresh cilantro

1. To prepare harissa, in a small bowl, combine oil, garlic, paprika, cumin, salt and cayenne. Rub into lamb.
2. Heat a large heavy skillet over medium-high heat. Cook racks, meaty side down, for 1 to 2 minutes, or until browned. Transfer to a parchment-lined baking sheet, bone side down, and roast in a preheated 400°F (200°C) oven for 20 to 25 minutes, or until a meat thermometer registers 135°F (57°C).
3. To prepare drizzle, in a bowl, combine mayonnaise, garlic, lemon juice, hot pepper sauce, cumin, paprika and cilantro. Taste and adjust seasonings if necessary.
4. Slice lamb into individual chops and drizzle with charmoula.

MAKES 10 TO 12 SERVINGS

Roasted Tzimmes

There are as many recipes for tzimmes as there are cooks who make it, but most are sweet and include carrots, potatoes and meat.

For those who don't like the mushy texture of traditional tzimmes, here's a modern version from my friend Mitchell Davis. The vegetables are roasted so they keep their shape but still have the traditional flavors of cinnamon and honey. And, as a bonus, the dish is vegetarian.

3 lb (1.5 kg) sweet potatoes, peeled and cut in wedges
3 lb (1.5 kg) carrots, cut in 2-inch (5 cm) pieces on diagonal
1 lb (500 g) onions, peeled and cut in wedges
½ cup (125 mL) prunes
¼ cup (50 mL) extra-virgin olive oil
¼ cup (50 mL) honey
¼ cup (50 mL) orange juice
2 tsp (10 mL) kosher salt
½ tsp (2 mL) pepper
½ tsp (2 mL) ground cinnamon
2 tbsp (25 mL) chopped fresh parsley

1. In a large bowl, combine sweet potatoes, carrots, onions and prunes.
2. In a small bowl, combine oil, honey, orange juice, salt, pepper and cinnamon. Add to vegetables and toss.
3. Spread veggies in a single layer on two parchment-lined baking sheets. Cover with foil.
4. Roast vegetables in a preheated 400°F (200°C) oven for 25 minutes. Uncover and continue to roast for 20 to 25 minutes, or until browned.
5. Serve vegetables sprinkled with parsley.

MAKES 10 TO 12 SERVINGS

Mixed Greens with Sweet Israeli Dressing

Salads are fabulous in Israel. This dressing comes from Olive and Fish restaurant in Jerusalem. The last time we visited, everyone wanted the recipe for this salad dressing, so here's what I came up with from the list of ingredients they gave me.

This is enough dressing for about 20 cups (5 L) of greens—enough to serve about 18 to 20 people—so just use what you need (I don't use too much, but just toss and toss until all the lettuce is coated).

If you are not making this at Passover, add 2 tsp (10 mL) Dijon mustard.

1 clove garlic, minced
½ tsp (2 mL) finely chopped fresh ginger
1 tsp (5 mL) kosher salt
¼ tsp (1 mL) pepper
1 tbsp (15 mL) honey
2 tbsp (25 mL) brown sugar
1 ½ tbsp (22 mL) apple juice concentrate
¼ cup (50 mL) white or red wine vinegar
½ cup (125 mL) extra-virgin olive oil
1 large head Boston lettuce, torn in pieces
1 large head Romaine lettuce, torn in pieces
1 red-tipped leaf lettuce, torn in pieces
2 Belgian endives, separated in leaves

1. In a bowl, whisk together garlic, ginger, salt, pepper, honey, sugar, apple juice concentrate, vinegar and oil. Taste and adjust seasonings if necessary.
2. Combine lettuces and endives in a large bowl. Just before serving, toss with just enough dressing to coat leaves.

MAKES 10 TO 12 SERVINGS

Clementine Cake with Chocolate Glaze

I first had this cake at the home of Rick Halpern, principal of New College (my alma mater at the University of Toronto), and his wife, Beth Landau. Serve it on its own, with the chocolate glaze, or with a non-dairy chocolate glaze (page 255). It also freezes well.

    The cake is perfectly delicious for any occasion but works well for Passover because it contains no flour. (Certain brands of baking powder have been "cleared" for Passover use; check with your local authority.)

    1 lb (500 g) whole clementines (about 4) or oranges (about 2)
    6 eggs
    1 cup (250 mL) granulated sugar
    2 cups (500 mL) ground toasted almonds
    1 tsp (5 mL) baking powder, optional

    CHOCOLATE GLAZE (OPTIONAL)
    6 oz (175 g) semisweet or bittersweet chocolate, chopped
    ¼ cup (50 mL) butter

1. Place whole clementines in a large pot and cover with water. Bring to a boil. Simmer for 2 hours, adding water if necessary to keep fruit covered. (Place a plate on top of oranges to hold them down.) Cool. Cut clementines in pieces and remove seeds. Place everything (peel, pith and pulp) in a food processor and process until smooth.

2. In a large bowl, beat eggs and sugar until very light.

3. In a separate bowl, combine almonds and baking powder, if using. Stir into batter. Add clementine puree. (Or, mix the whole thing in a large food processor by adding 2 eggs at a time to puree. Combine sugar with nuts and baking powder in a bowl, add to egg mixture and process until combined.)

4. Transfer batter to a 9-inch (23 cm) springform pan that has been oiled, lined with parchment and oiled again. Bake in a preheated 350°F (180°C) oven for 35 to 40 minutes, or until set. If cake starts to brown too much, cover loosely with foil during baking. Cool cake and remove from pan.

5. Meanwhile, if you are making glaze, combine chocolate and butter in top of a double boiler or in a microwave. Stir until smooth. Cool slightly. Pour or spread over cake.

MAKES 10 TO 12 SERVINGS

Chocolate Meringue Kisses

These sweet little rosettes, inspired by talented pastry chef and cookbook author Nick Malgieri, are a great alternative to macaroons. They should be crisp on the outside and slightly chewy on the inside. They freeze well.

> 3 egg whites
> ⅞ cup (200 mL) granulated sugar
> 3 oz (100 g) unsweetened or semisweet chocolate, melted and cooled

1. Whisk egg whites and sugar together in a large bowl.
2. Bring a saucepan of water to a boil and place bowl of egg whites on top. Stir until sugar dissolves and egg whites are very warm.
3. Remove from heat and beat egg whites with an electric mixer until they are cool and shiny. Fold in cooled melted chocolate.
4. Place mixture in a piping tube fitted with a ½-inch (1 cm) star nozzle and pipe rosettes (or mound with a spoon) onto a parchment-lined baking sheet.
5. Bake in a preheated 300°F (150°C) oven for 10 to 12 minutes, or until meringues are firm outside but still chewy inside.

MAKES 24 COOKIES

Caramel Matzah Crunch

My Passover would not be complete without this, but you don't have to wait for Passover or even be Jewish to love it. It is irresistible.

Although I have now seen the recipe in many places (I think it was originally made with Graham crackers), Marcy Goldman, a terrific Montreal baker and cookbook author, takes credit for inventing it.

There are lots of variations. You can use milk or white chocolate instead of semisweet or swirl them together. You can even omit the chocolate altogether and sprinkle 2 cups (500 mL) sliced almonds over the caramel topping before baking.

> 6 pieces regular matzah (about 7 x 6 inches/ 18 x 15 cm)
> 1 cup (250 mL) packed brown sugar
> 1 cup (250 mL) butter or margarine
> 2 cups (500 mL) chopped semisweet chocolate (or chocolate chips)

1. Line a large (18- x 12-inch/45 x 30 cm) baking sheet with foil. Arrange matzah in a single layer on foil; don't worry if pieces overlap.
2. Combine sugar and butter in a saucepan and bring to a boil. Do not stir. Cook for a few minutes, or until mixture comes together and does not look oily. Pour mixture over matzah as evenly as possible.
3. Bake in a preheated 350°F (180°C) oven for 10 to 12 minutes, or until mixture is bubbling.
4. As soon as matzah comes out of oven, sprinkle with chocolate. Let chocolate melt for about 5 minutes. With a knife, spread chocolate as evenly as possible.
5. Chill until chocolate and caramel are set. Break into uneven chunks.

THERE'S NEVER ENOUGH!

ROASTED CAULIFLOWER WITH TAHINA

FALAFEL

ROAST CHICKEN ON A RACK

ROASTED BRUSSELS SPROUTS

CREAMY MASHED POTATOES

CHOCOLATIEST CHOCOLATE CHIP COOKIES

CHUCK'S CHOCOLATE BROWNIES

dinner with chuck

SERVES 6

It is hard to imagine the relief we felt when my nephew, Corporal Chuck Krangle (shown with Major Trevor Cadieu on the left) came home safely from serving with the Canadian Forces in Afghanistan. When you actually know someone overseas, every newscast, every article, every battle and every loss becomes very personal.

I would have cooked him anything when he returned, but all he wanted was his favorite dinner from when he was a kid—roast chicken. Really simple, but something we all love.

While he was away, we sent him cookies every few weeks and discovered which ones traveled best. Brownies and chocolate chip cookies were a big hit, and usually arrived intact. When he told me they often disappeared before he could finish opening the parcel, I wanted to cry.

The cauliflower, falafel and cookies can all be made ahead. Roast the chicken and Brussels sprouts in the oven together while you are making the mashed potatoes.

Roasted Cauliflower with Tahina

I first had something like this at my favorite Middle Eastern restaurant in Toronto, Tabülè. They deep-fry the cauliflower and it's delicious that way, but I like to roast it.

Serve this as an appetizer (place a toothpick in each floret) or side dish. The sauce is good on any roasted or grilled vegetable, or you can use it for dipping. Serve at room temperature or reheat.

1 large head cauliflower, broken in florets
2 tbsp (25 mL) extra-virgin olive oil
1 tsp (5 mL) kosher salt

TAHINA SAUCE
½ cup (125 mL) tahina
1 clove garlic, minced
¼ cup (50 mL) lemon juice
1 tsp (5 mL) kosher salt
Dash hot red pepper sauce
½ cup (125 mL) water, approx.

1. In a large bowl, combine cauliflower, oil and salt. Spread in a single layer on a parchment-lined baking sheet. Roast in a preheated 400°F (200°C) oven for 25 to 35 minutes, or until browned.
2. Meanwhile, to prepare tahina sauce, in a bowl, whisk tahina, garlic, lemon juice, salt and hot pepper sauce. Whisk in water until sauce turns white and can be drizzled.
3. Drizzle cauliflower with tahina sauce or serve the sauce as a dip.

MAKES 6 SERVINGS

Falafel

Falafel are the pin-up Middle Eastern food. They are easy to make as long as you remember to soak the chickpeas the night before. Soak lots of chickpeas and freeze them so that you can have speedier falafel the next time. (You could also use canned, but the texture will not be as good.)

Serve these hot as an appetizer or main course, either on their own or in pita sandwiches with tahina sauce and salsa. They also make very cute appetizers served in tiny pitas.

1½ cups (375 mL) dried chickpeas
3 cloves garlic, peeled
1 small onion, coarsely chopped
3 tbsp (45 mL) panko or fresh breadcrumbs
1 tbsp (15 mL) ground cumin (preferably toasted)
1 tbsp (15 mL) ground coriander
1 tsp (5 mL) kosher salt
¼ tsp (1 mL) cayenne, hot red pepper sauce or aleppo pepper
¼ cup (50 mL) chopped fresh cilantro
¼ cup (50 mL) vegetable oil
Tahina Sauce (page 194)
Tomato Lime Salsa (page 65)

1. In a large bowl, cover chickpeas generously with cold water. Refrigerate overnight. Drain well.
2. In a food processor, chop garlic and onion until very fine. Add uncooked soaked chickpeas, breadcrumbs, cumin, coriander, salt and cayenne and pulse on/off until mixture starts to get pasty and holds together when you pinch it. Add cilantro and process on/off until finely chopped.
3. With a generous tablespoon, shape mixture into about 30 balls and flatten slightly.
4. Heat oil in a large skillet over medium-high heat. Add falafel and cook for 3 to 4 minutes per side, or until crispy. Drain on paper towels. Repeat until all are cooked. Serve with sauce and/or salsa.

MAKES ABOUT 30 FALAFEL

Roast Chicken on a Rack

There is nothing easier, more comforting or more popular than a good roast chicken. The quality of the bird is the most important factor, so try to find an organic or naturally raised chicken.

My favorite way to roast a chicken is on a chicken stand (it looks a little like a model of the Eiffel Tower). If you don't have a stand (they are very inexpensive and easily available), you can follow the advice of Steven Raichlen (author of *The Barbecue Bible*) and substitute a beer can. In either case, remove the top rack of your oven and place the other rack in the lowest position. I like to place the chicken over a mound of salt. I have no idea why it makes the chicken so tasty, but it does. (Of course you can just roast the chicken on a wire rack in a roasting pan, but it is not nearly as much fun.)

You can also brush the chicken with olive oil, dust it with spice rubs or fresh herbs, or smear mixtures under the skin, but if I have a good chicken, I like it cooked simply with salt and pepper. Roast vegetables around the chicken if you wish.

> 1 3- to 4-lb (1.5 to 2 kg) whole chicken
> Salt and pepper to taste

1. Line a baking sheet with parchment paper or foil. If you are using a chicken stand, mound about 1 cup (250 mL) kosher salt in middle of pan. Place stand on top of salt and impale chicken on stand (salt shouldn't touch chicken). If you are using a beer can, omit salt, drink or discard about half the beer and carefully place can on baking sheet. Impale chicken on can.
2. Season chicken generously with salt and pepper.
3. Place baking sheet on bottom rack of a preheated 400°F (200°C) oven. Roast chicken for 1 to 1¼ hours, or until cooked through and well browned. A meat thermometer should read 165°F (75°C) when inserted into thigh.
4. Remove chicken from stand or beer can very carefully, using heavy-duty rubber gloves or tea towels. (If using beer can, make sure hot beer does not spill onto your hands.) Cut chicken into serving pieces.

MAKES 6 SERVINGS

Roasted Brussels Sprouts

Some people think they don't like Brussels sprouts, but once again, roasting comes to the rescue. If you are roasting these with the chicken, arrange the sprouts around the chicken about halfway through the roasting time.

1½ lb (750 g) Brussels sprouts
2 tbsp (25 mL) extra-virgin olive oil
1 tbsp (15 mL) fresh thyme leaves, or ½ tsp (2 mL) dried
1 tsp (5 mL) kosher salt
½ tsp (2 mL) pepper

1. Trim sprouts and cut in half if they are large.
2. In a large bowl, combine sprouts, oil, thyme, salt and pepper.
3. Transfer sprouts to a parchment-lined baked sheet and roast in a preheated 400°F (200°C) oven for 30 to 40 minutes, or until browned and tender.

MAKES 6 SERVINGS

Creamy Mashed Potatoes

Chuck wanted mashed potatoes. This is as comforting as it gets. They'll stay warm in a covered pot for up to an hour before serving.

If you wish, use half sweet potatoes and half regular potatoes, but reduce the amount of liquid slightly. You can also add fresh chives, roasted garlic, dill or tarragon.

For the creamiest mashed potatoes, use a food mill or potato ricer. For a "country mash" texture, mash with a potato masher, but never use a food processor, which will make the potatoes pastelike.

2 lb (1 kg) Yukon gold potatoes or baking potatoes (about 3 large)
½ cup (125 mL) hot milk, cream, soy milk, stock or potato-cooking liquid, approx.
¼ cup (50 mL) butter or extra-virgin olive oil
1 tsp (5 mL) kosher salt
¼ tsp (1 mL) pepper

1. Peel potatoes and cut into 2-inch (5 cm) chunks. Place potatoes in a saucepan of salted water. Bring to a boil and cook until tender, about 20 minutes. Drain well and return to pot.
2. Mash in hot liquid, butter, salt and pepper. Taste and adjust seasonings if necessary.

MAKES 6 SERVINGS

Chocolatiest Chocolate Chip Cookies

I like to use Valrhona chocolate discs in cookies. Then I don't have to chop the chocolate as much—I usually just cut them in half or thirds.

I usually make large cookies with ¼ cup (50 mL) batter. They end up about 4 inches (10 cm) in diameter. You can also make them smaller (about 2 tbsp/25 mL batter each), but they will be a bit crisper and not quite as chewy as the larger ones.

1 cup (500 mL) butter or margarine
¾ cup (175 mL) granulated sugar
1¼ cups (300 mL) packed brown sugar
2 eggs
2 tsp (10 mL) vanilla paste or pure vanilla extract
3 cups (750 mL) all-purpose flour
1½ tsp (7 mL) kosher salt
1 tsp (5 mL) baking powder
1 tsp (5 mL) baking soda
12 oz (375 g) semisweet, bittersweet or milk chocolate (or a combination), chopped

1. In a food processor or with an electric mixer, cream butter with sugars until smooth and creamy. Beat in eggs one at a time. Beat in vanilla.
2. In a large bowl, mix together flour, salt, baking powder and baking soda.
3. Stir butter mixture into dry ingredients and knead together with a wooden spoon or your hands. Stir in chocolate.
4. Using a ¼ cup (50 mL) measuring cup or ice cream scoop for each cookie, place batter on parchment-lined baking sheets about 2 inches (5 cm) apart. Bake in a preheated 350°F (180°C) oven for 12 to 16 minutes, or until tops are browned and cookies are slightly puffed (they will fall and become wrinkled when they cool). Cool on wire racks.

MAKES ABOUT 18 TO 20 LARGE COOKIES OR 36 TO 40 SMALLER ONES

Chuck's Chocolate Brownies

Although we keep trying new brownie recipes just in case, these have been our favorites for years. For a plated dessert, serve larger squares with ice cream (dairy or non-dairy) and chocolate sauce.

> 10 oz (300 g) bittersweet or semisweet chocolate, chopped
>
> 1 cup (250 mL) butter or vegetable oil
>
> 4 eggs
>
> 2 cups (500 mL) granulated sugar
>
> 1 tsp (5 mL) vanilla paste or pure vanilla extract
>
> 1 cup (250 mL) all-purpose flour
>
> 1 tsp (5 mL) baking powder
>
> 2 cups (500 mL) chopped toasted pecans, chopped chocolate
> (white, milk or dark) or a combination

1. Heat chocolate and butter in a heavy saucepan over low heat. Stir until combined. Cool.
2. In a large bowl, whisk eggs and sugar. Beat in vanilla and melted chocolate mixture.
3. In a separate bowl, combine flour and baking powder. Add to egg mixture and stir just until mixed in. Stir in nuts.
4. Spread batter evenly in a 13- x 9-inch (3 L) oiled and parchment-lined baking dish. Bake in a preheated 350°F (180°C) oven for 25 to 30 minutes, or until brownies are firm on the outside but still moist inside. Do not overbake or brownies will be cake-like instead of chewy. Cool in pan on a rack and chill until firm. Lift out of pan and trim edges before cutting into squares.

MAKES 30 LARGE BROWNIES

Chocolate Sauce

In a small, heavy saucepan, combine 4 oz (125 g) chopped semisweet chocolate, 2 tbsp (25 mL) cocoa, 2 tbsp (25 mL) corn syrup and ⅔ cup (150 mL) water or milk. Heat gently, stirring until smooth. Stir in 2 tsp (10 mL) vanilla and 2 tbsp (25 mL) butter (optional). Serve warm or at room temperature.

Makes 1¼ cups (300 mL).

SPARKLING GREEN TEA AND LYCHEE SANGRIA

CHICKEN DUMPLINGS WITH THAI PEANUT SAUCE

ROASTED HALIBUT WITH GREEN CURRY COCONUT SAUCE

CILANTRO RICE PILAF

OR

SPICED BASMATI RICE

STIR-FRIED BABY BOK CHOY

COCONUT RICE PUDDING

asian dinner

SERVES 8

Fusion cooking has come to mean many things. The over-the-top style of combining cuisines has gone out of fashion, but there are still delicious ways to mix and match techniques and flavors from different countries. And in fact there is really nothing new about that anyway; whenever people emigrate they create fusion food by adapting their traditional cuisine to local ingredients.

Here's an Asian-inspired menu that has exciting flavors but is easy to make, with readily accessible ingredients.

Some of this menu can be prepared ahead—the base for the sangria, the sauce for the fish and the dessert. You can also cook the dumplings ahead, but combine them with the sauce just before serving.

Sparkling Green Tea and Lychee Sangria

For a non-alcoholic version, use soda water or ginger ale instead of the sparkling wine, and orange juice concentrate instead of the liqueur. If you can't find lychee juice, just use another light-colored juice such as white cranberry.

1 ½ cups (375 mL) water
3 green tea teabags, or 1 tbsp (15 mL) green tea leaves
¼ cup (50 mL) granulated sugar, or ⅓ cup (75 mL) sugar syrup (page 86)
¾ cup (175 mL) lychee juice
¾ cup (175 mL) pineapple juice
2 tbsp (25 mL) lychee or orange liqueur, optional
3 cups (750 mL) sparkling white wine (e.g., Prosecco or Cava)
Ice cubes

1. In a saucepan, bring water to a boil. Add tea and sugar and stir well. Remove from heat and steep for at least 30 minutes.
2. Strain tea and add juices and liqueur, if using. Refrigerate.
3. Just before serving, add sparkling wine. Serve over ice.

MAKES 8 TO 10 SERVINGS

Chicken Dumplings with Thai Peanut Sauce

I always credit Hugh Carpenter, one of our favorite visiting chefs, for bringing dumplings into our lives. They seem complicated—until you make your first batch. Once you realize how easy they are, you'll make them all the time. We constantly reinvent them with different fillings or different sauces, but we never stop making them. They can be frozen before cooking as long as the meat and/or fish in the filling has not been previously frozen. Or you can cook them and then freeze. Sprinkle them with chopped cilantro or roasted peanuts before serving if you wish.

Add the sauce to the dumplings just before serving, as it can separate if overheated (if it does, don't worry; the dish will still taste delicious).

1 lb (500 g) ground chicken

1 egg white

1 tbsp (15 mL) cornstarch

1 tsp (5 mL) kosher salt

1 small jalapeño, seeded and finely chopped

½ cup (125 mL) chopped fresh cilantro

35 square Chinese wonton wrappers

1 tbsp (15 mL) vegetable oil

½ cup (125 mL) water

PEANUT SAUCE

½ cup (125 mL) coconut milk

¼ cup (50 mL) water

3 tbsp (45 mL) smooth peanut butter

1 tbsp (15 mL) soy sauce

2 tsp (10 mL) red Thai curry paste

2 tsp (10 mL) granulated sugar

1. In a bowl or food processor, combine chicken, egg white, cornstarch, salt, jalapeño and cilantro.

2. Arrange wonton wrappers on work surface (you may have to do this in batches) in a single layer. Place about 1½ tsp (7 mL) filling in center of each wrapper.

3. Bring sides of wrapper up around filling, leaving top open. Squeeze lightly around middle to give dumpling a "waist." Flatten dumpling gently and place open side up on a lightly oiled waxed paper–lined baking sheet. Continue until all filling is used. Refrigerate.

4. To prepare sauce, whisk coconut milk, water, peanut butter, soy sauce, curry paste and sugar.

5. To cook, heat oil in a nonstick skillet over medium-high heat. Arrange dumplings open side up in skillet. Cook for about 2 minutes, or until lightly browned on bottom.

6. Add water. Cover, reduce heat and cook for 3 to 5 minutes, or until filling is firm when pressed, and water has been absorbed. Remove from heat. Over very gentle heat, add sauce and combine just until sauce coats dumplings.

MAKES 35 DUMPLINGS

Roasted Halibut with Green Curry Coconut Sauce

Commercial curry pastes can vary in heat, so be careful not to use too much if you are unfamiliar with the brand. Taste a bit first. Also, if you don't eat shellfish, read the labels carefully, as some commercial curry pastes contain fish sauce and/or shrimp paste. In that case, make your own.

This sauce tastes fantastic served with salmon, lamb chops, chicken and shrimp. It can also be made with red curry paste.

You can saute or grill individual pieces of halibut, but it is easier to roast a larger piece, so that's what I usually do. For a lovely presentation that isn't too much work, buy frozen banana leaves at an Asian store. They are very inexpensive. Defrost and wipe them clean and cut them in wide strips to fit across each plate. I like to place some rice on the leaf, top with bok choy and the fish and then spoon sauce over the top.

GREEN CURRY COCONUT SAUCE
2 tbsp (25 mL) vegetable oil
1 tbsp (15 mL) chopped fresh ginger
1 tbsp (15 mL) chopped fresh lemongrass
½ cup (125 mL) fresh basil
1 tbsp (15 mL) green Thai curry paste
1 cup (250 mL) coconut milk
1 tbsp (15 mL) sweet Thai chili sauce
¼ cup (50 mL) fresh cilantro
1 tbsp (15 mL) soy sauce
1 tbsp (15 mL) granulated sugar
1 tbsp (15 mL) lime juice
Salt and pepper to taste

ROASTED HALIBUT
3 lb (1.5 L) halibut fillet (in 1 or 2 large pieces), without skin
Salt and pepper to taste

1. To prepare sauce, heat oil in a large saucepan. Add ginger, lemongrass, basil and curry paste and cook, stirring, for a few minutes.

2. Add coconut milk, sweet chili sauce and cilantro. Bring almost to a boil, reduce heat and cook gently for 15 minutes. Strain sauce and return to saucepan.

3. Add soy sauce, sugar and lime juice. Season with salt and pepper.

4. To prepare halibut, season fish with salt and pepper. Place on a parchment-lined baking sheet. Spread one-third of sauce over fish. Roast in a preheated 425°F (220°C) oven for 15 to 20 minutes, or until just cooked.

5. Heat remaining sauce and spoon over fish when serving.

MAKES 8 SERVINGS

Green Curry Paste

This recipe comes from Linda Stephen. She has taught at my school for many years and has her own cooking school in Cobourg, Ontario. This recipe is from her book, *Complete Book of Thai Cooking*. Unlike most commercial curry pastes, it contains no shrimp paste. For a milder paste, reduce the number of chilies. Freeze any extra paste.

In a food processor, combine 3 tbsp (45 mL) coarsely chopped fresh green chilies, 1 stalk coarsely chopped lemongrass (white part only), 5 coarsely chopped shallots, 4 peeled garlic cloves, 1 tbsp (15 mL) chopped galangal or fresh ginger, 1 torn lime leaf (vein removed), 3 tbsp (45 mL) coarsely chopped fresh cilantro roots and stems and ¼ cup (50 mL) water.

Add ½ tsp (2 mL) each ground coriander, ground cumin and pepper. Blend until a paste forms, scraping down sides of food processor. Add extra water 1 tsp (5 mL) at a time if necessary.

Makes about ¾ cup (175 mL).

Cilantro Rice Pilaf

You can also make this with brown rice or wehani rice—just double the cooking time and use 4 cups (1 L) water. Use the cilantro stems as well as the leaves to make the puree.

    2 tbsp (25 mL) extra-virgin olive oil
    1 large onion, chopped
    2 cloves garlic, finely chopped
    2 cups (500 mL) long-grain rice, preferably basmati or jasmine, rinsed
    3½ cups (875 mL) vegetable stock or water, divided
    1 tsp (5 mL) kosher salt
    ¼ tsp (1 mL) pepper
    1 small bunch fresh cilantro

1. Heat oil in a saucepan over medium heat. Add onion and garlic and cook, stirring, for a few minutes, or until soft. Add rice and stir into onions well.
2. Add 3¼ cups (800 mL) stock, salt and pepper. Bring to a boil, cover and cook for 15 to 20 minutes, or until rice is tender and liquid has been absorbed.
3. Meanwhile, puree cilantro with remaining ¼ cup (50 mL) stock in a blender or food processor. Stir gently into cooked rice. Taste and adjust seasonings if necessary.

MAKES 8 SERVINGS

Spiced Basmati Rice

If you make this with brown basmati, use an extra ½ cup (125 mL) liquid and cook for 45 to 50 minutes.

> 2 cups (500 mL) basmati rice
> 1 tbsp (15 mL) vegetable oil
> 1 cinnamon stick, broken in 2 or 3 pieces
> 3 whole cloves
> 4 cardamom pods
> 1 onion, chopped
> 1 clove garlic, finely chopped
> 3 cups (750 mL) water
> Salt and pepper to taste

1. Rinse rice in a sieve until water runs clear. Drain very well.
2. Heat oil in a large saucepan. Add cinnamon, cloves and cardamom. Cook for 30 to 60 seconds, or until very fragrant.
3. Add onion and garlic. Cook for a few minutes, or until softened.
4. Add rice and stir to coat well with onion and spices. Add water and bring to a boil. Season with salt and pepper, cover and simmer gently over low heat for 15 to 20 minutes, or until rice is tender.
5. Stir gently and adjust seasonings to taste. Discard spices or warn guests not to eat them.

MAKES 8 SERVINGS

Stir-fried Baby Bok Choy

Bok choy has become a very popular vegetable. Even kids love it. Use it in stir-fries or serve it on its own as a side dish like this one. If you can't find baby bok choy, use larger ones and cut them in half.

    1 tbsp (15 mL) vegetable oil
    1 clove garlic, finely chopped
    1 ½ lb (750 g) baby bok choy
    2 tbsp (25 mL) soy sauce
    ¼ cup (50 mL) water

1. Heat oil in a wok or large deep skillet over medium-high heat. Add garlic and cook for about 10 seconds. Do not brown.
2. Add bok choy and stir-fry for 1 minute.
3. Add soy sauce and water and bring to a boil. Cook for about 5 minutes, stirring often, until bok choy wilts slightly and becomes tender.

MAKES 8 SERVINGS

Coconut Rice Pudding

At the cooking school, this is our favorite treat that Dely Balagtas makes for us. It is completely different from Western versions of rice pudding. It uses coconut milk—great for people like my husband, Ray, who loves rice pudding but is lactose intolerant (though Ray prefers it without the ginger).

Serve this on its own, on top of grilled pineapple (page 167) or surrounded with fresh mango slices.

> 1 cup (250 mL) sticky rice or short-grain rice (or a combination)
> 1½ cups (375 mL) cold water
> ½ cup (125 mL) granulated sugar
> 1½ cups (375 mL) coconut milk
> 2 tbsp (25 mL) chopped candied ginger, or 1 tbsp (15 mL) grated fresh ginger, optional
> 1 tsp (5 mL) vanilla paste or pure vanilla extract

1. Rinse rice in two changes of water only.
2. In a saucepan, combine rice and cold water and bring to a boil. Cover, reduce heat and cook gently for 15 minutes.
3. Meanwhile, in a saucepan, cook sugar, without stirring, over medium-high heat for 5 to 7 minutes, or until sugar melts and turns golden brown. Do not burn. Remove from heat.
4. Standing back, add coconut milk to sugar. Do not worry if mixture bubbles furiously and sugar hardens. Cook gently until mixture smoothes out.
5. Add rice and ginger, if using. Cover and cook over very low heat for 10 minutes, or until very creamy. Stir in vanilla. Serve warm or cold.

MAKES 8 SERVINGS

MARINATED GOAT CHEESE

GRILLED GARLIC BREAD

SALMON PICCATA WITH LEMON AND ASPARAGUS

ROASTED POTATO STICKS

AFFOGATO

fast food fish

SERVES 6

Fish is the ultimate fast food. When students ask me how to cook fish in the microwave, I realize that most people don't understand how quickly fish really cooks—10 minutes per inch of thickness over medium-high or high heat.

This is a very easy menu to put together, even if you have been working all day and are cooking dinner at the last minute, though the goat cheese can be prepared in advance. You can prepare the garlic bread ahead, too, and grill it just before serving. And as long as you have chocolate brownies on hand—either store-bought or homemade (page 201) they freeze perfectly—you can whip up this sexy Italian dessert.

Marinated Goat Cheese

Marinated goat cheese is a quick appetizer that never loses its appeal. It will keep for at least a week in the refrigerator (bring to room temperature before serving).

To slice the goat cheese easily into rounds, use dental floss.

12 oz (375 g) goat cheese, cut in rounds ½ inch (1 cm) thick
1 tbsp (15 mL) fresh thyme
1 tbsp (15 mL) chopped fresh rosemary
1 tsp (5 mL) pepper
2 cloves garlic, minced
1 tbsp (15 mL) aged balsamic vinegar
⅓ cup (75 mL) extra-virgin olive oil

1. Arrange slices of goat cheese in a single layer in a serving dish.
2. Sprinkle thyme, rosemary, pepper and garlic over cheese. Drizzle with vinegar and oil. Marinate for up to a few hours at room temperature or refrigerate.

MAKES 6 SERVINGS

Grilled Garlic Bread

Everyone in my family loves this garlic bread. Use it as a base for spreads like marinated goat cheese or serve it on its own. Chopped fresh rosemary, thyme and pepper are great additions, too. I also like this made with rye bread, black bread or pita.

¼ cup (50 mL) extra-virgin olive oil (or half butter, half olive oil)
2 cloves garlic, minced
1 tsp (5 mL) kosher salt
12 slices baguette, cut on diagonal in slices ½ inch (1 cm) thick

1. In a small bowl, combine oil, garlic and salt.
2. Brush oil mixture on one side of bread.
3. Just before serving, grill bread (on barbecue, or in a grill pan or sandwich press) for about 1 to 2 minutes per side, or until browned on each side. (You can also place bread on a baking sheet and bake in a preheated 400°F/200°C oven for 5 to 8 minutes, or until bread is crisp on the outside and chewy inside.)

MAKES 12 PIECES

Salmon Piccata with Lemon and Asparagus

I used to sauté thin slices of salmon for this recipe, but roasting a large fillet is much easier. I usually use a large spoon to break the fish into serving pieces at the table, but if you prefer a tidier presentation, you can cut the salmon into serving pieces before cooking and press them back together so the fish will stay juicy.

Halibut is also delicious cooked like this.

> 1 2-lb (1 kg) boneless, skinless salmon fillet (preferably wild),
>   about 1½ inches (4 cm) thick
> 1½ lb (750 g) asparagus, trimmed
> 3 tbsp (45 mL) extra-virgin olive oil
> 1 tbsp (15 mL) grated lemon peel
> 1 tbsp (15 mL) chopped fresh rosemary or thyme, or 1 tsp (5 mL) dried
> 1 tsp (5 mL) kosher salt
> ¼ tsp (1 mL) pepper
> 3 tbsp (45 mL) butter, divided
> 1 small shallot, finely chopped
> 2 tbsp (25 mL) lemon juice
> 1 tbsp (15 mL) capers, rinsed and drained
> Salt and pepper to taste
> 2 tbsp (25 mL) chopped fresh parsley

1. Place salmon on a parchment-lined baking sheet. Cut asparagus in half on diagonal if you wish.
2. In a small bowl, combine oil, lemon peel, rosemary, salt and pepper. Brush most of mixture over salmon and toss remainder with asparagus. If asparagus is thick, place it on baking sheet beside or around salmon, but if it is thin, add it 10 minutes after salmon goes into oven.
3. Place salmon (and thick asparagus) in a preheated 400°F (200°C) oven and cook just until fish comes apart, about 15 to 18 minutes, depending on thickness of salmon. Be sure not to overcook fish.
4. Meanwhile, melt 1 tbsp (15 mL) butter in a small saucepan over medium heat. Add shallot and cook for 2 to 3 minutes, or until tender.
5. Add lemon juice and capers. Season with salt and pepper. Remove from heat and stir in remaining 2 tbsp (25 mL) butter.
6. Transfer salmon and asparagus to a serving platter. Spoon sauce over salmon and sprinkle with parsley.

MAKES 6 SERVINGS

Roasted Potato Sticks

These make a great appetizer served with garlic mayonnaise (page 173) or truffle salt. Or you can make your own poutine using leftover shredded brisket (page 88-89) or shortribs (page 8). Add grated cheese if you wish. For a spicier variation, use 3 tbsp (45 mL) vegetable oil, 1 tbsp (15 mL) curry paste and ½ tsp (7 mL) kosher salt.

> 3 lb (1.5 kg) Yukon Gold or baking potatoes,
>   peeled and cut in sticks about ½ inch (1 cm) thick
> 3 tbsp (45 mL) extra-virgin olive oil
> 1½ tsp (7 mL) kosher salt
> 1 tsp (5 mL) paprika
> 2 tbsp (25 mL) fresh thyme, or 1 tsp (5 mL) dried

1. In a large bowl, toss potatoes, oil, salt, paprika and thyme. Spread on a parchment-lined baking sheet.
2. Roast in a preheated 400°F (200°C) oven for about 45 minutes, or until browned and tender. Toss a few times during cooking if you wish.

MAKES 6 SERVINGS

Affogato

Most of the time affogato ("to drown") just refers to ice cream with a shot of espresso on top, but at the Barevo Espresso Bar in Sydney, Australia, the barista showed me how to make this deluxe version. Each shot is two tablespoons (1 oz/30 g), so you will need ¾ cup (175 mL) espresso for six desserts. Use storebought or homemade brownies.

You can also just serve the brownies and ice cream with chocolate sauce (page 201) and call them brownie sundaes.

6 mini brownies (page 201)
6 mini scoops vanilla ice cream
¾ cup (175 mL) hot espresso or very strong coffee

1. Place brownies in shot glasses or small bowls.
2. Place a mini scoop of ice cream on each brownie.
3. Pour a shot of espresso over each serving. Serve with a small spoon.

MAKES 6 SERVINGS

WILD MUSHROOM MINI STRUDELS
GREEK SALAD IN CUCUMBER BASKETS WITH GRILLED PITA
SWORDFISH SOUVLAKI WITH LEMON DRESSING
MEDITERRANEAN RICE PILAF
GREEK WEDDING COOKIES
LEMON YOGURT CAKE WITH LEMON GLAZE

greek dinner

SERVES 6 TO 8

When we featured *Toronto Life* writer James Chatto's wonderful memoir, *The Greek for Love*, at our book club, we served many of the dishes in this menu, and I have to say we were quite nervous, because James has such a discerning palate. We were extremely relieved when he did in fact eat everything!

You can please your toughest critic with this menu, too. I like to serve the main course on a large platter. I place the skewers on top of the rice, sprinkle the tomatoes and olives on top and then drizzle the lemon dressing and tzatziki over everything.

Most of the dishes can be prepared ahead—the mini strudels, the cookies and cake (make one or both desserts), as well as the salad dressing and tzatziki for the souvlaki.

Wild Mushroom Mini Strudels

Everyone loves appetizers made with phyllo pastry. This is an easy version of Greek spanakopita because you shape the pastries into rolls rather than fussy triangles. The mini rolls are nice and crusty and can easily be cut into bite-sized pieces.

Don't bother using large portobellos in recipes where the mushrooms are just going to be chopped. Use the smaller and less expensive creminis. The dried wild mushrooms will add a lot of flavor.

These freeze well cooked or uncooked. Bake them from the frozen state (they will only take an extra 5 to 10 minutes to cook).

½ oz (15 g) dried wild mushrooms

1 cup (250 mL) hot water

1 tbsp (15 mL) extra-virgin olive oil

1 small onion, finely chopped

2 cloves garlic, finely chopped

2 lb (1 kg) cremini (brown button) mushrooms, chopped

8 oz (250 g) goat cheese, crumbled

2 eggs, beaten

3 tbsp (45 mL) chopped fresh tarragon or parsley

1 tsp (5 mL) kosher salt

½ tsp (2 mL) pepper

12 oz (375 g) phyllo pastry (12 sheets)

½ cup (125 mL) panko or dry breadcrumbs

⅓ cup (75 mL) melted butter or extra-virgin olive oil

1. Place dried mushrooms in a small bowl and cover with hot water. Soak for 30 minutes. Strain liquid through a sieve lined with a paper towel and reserve. Rinse mushrooms well and chop.

2. Heat oil in a large skillet over medium-high heat. Add onion and garlic and cook for a few minutes, or until tender and fragrant.

3. Add fresh and dried mushrooms and cook for a few minutes. Add reserved soaking liquid and cook mushrooms for about 10 minutes, or until all liquid evaporates. Cool completely.

4. In a large bowl, combine mushrooms and cheese. Stir in eggs, tarragon, salt and pepper. Combine well.

5. Unfold phyllo pastry and cover with plastic wrap and then with a damp tea towel. Place breadcrumbs and melted butter in two separate dishes.

6. Arrange one sheet of pastry on work surface. Brush with a little butter and sprinkle with breadcrumbs. Repeat with 2 more layers. Arrange 1 cup (250 mL) mushroom mixture down one long edge of pastry. Roll up lengthwise, tucking in ends as you roll. Transfer to a baking sheet and score top of pastry into 10 pieces with horizontal slashes (to make the rolls easier to slice later). Repeat until 4 rolls are made. Brush with any extra melted butter.

7. Bake in a preheated 400°F (200°C) oven 20 to 25 minutes, or until well browned. Slice and serve warm or at room temperature.

MAKES ABOUT 40 PIECES

Spinach and Feta Mini Strudels

Prepare filling by heating 1 tbsp (15 mL) extra-virgin olive oil in a small skillet over medium-high heat. Add 1 small chopped onion and 2 finely chopped garlic cloves and cook for a few minutes, or until tender and fragrant. Cool.

In a bowl, combine cooked onion mixture with 8 oz (250 g) crumbled feta cheese, 2 10-oz (300 g) packages frozen spinach (defrosted, squeezed dry and chopped), 2 beaten eggs, 3 tbsp (45 mL) chopped fresh dill, ½ tsp (2 mL) pepper and a pinch ground nutmeg.

Use instead of wild mushroom filling.

Greek Salad in Cucumber Baskets with Grilled Pita

This is a Greek salad with attitude. Leonie Eidinger, who works with me at the cooking school, came up with the clever idea of making cucumber baskets to present the salad. The grilled pita acts as croutons.

Sumac and za'atar can be found at Middle Eastern stores.

I am very fussy about using good feta cheese. I love the Greek feta I get from Ararat, my favorite Middle Eastern market in Toronto.

Serve this as an appetizer, or omit the cucumber baskets and serve as a side salad along with the main course.

2 cups (500 mL) cherry tomatoes
½ small English cucumber, peeled and diced
1 cup (250 mL) pitted black olives
8 oz (250 g) feta cheese, broken in large chunks
2 tbsp (25 mL) chopped fresh parsley
2 tbsp (25 mL) chopped fresh chives
2 tbsp (25 mL) chopped fresh cilantro
2 tbsp (25 mL) chopped fresh mint
2 tbsp (25 mL) lemon juice
1 clove garlic, minced
1 tsp (5 mL) dried oregano
1 tsp (5 mL) kosher salt
¼ tsp (1 mL) pepper
1 tsp (10 mL) sumac or za'atar, optional
½ cup (125 mL) extra-virgin olive oil
2 English cucumbers, whole
1 small head Romaine lettuce, cut in 1-inch (2.5 cm) chunks

GRILLED PITA
2 large pita breads
2 tbsp (25 mL) extra-virgin olive oil
2 tbsp (25 mL) za'atar or dried thyme

1. In a large bowl, combine tomatoes, diced cucumber, olives, feta and fresh herbs.
2. In a small bowl, whisk lemon juice, garlic, oregano, salt, pepper and sumac, if using. Whisk in oil. Add to tomato mixture and combine gently.
3. With a mandoline or cheese slicer, carefully cut wide strips down the length of the whole cucumbers. When you reach the seeds, cut strips from the other side. You will need 2 strips per serving.
4. Brush pitas with oil and sprinkle with za'atar. Grill pitas until browned. Cut into long thin strips or wedges. (You can also cut pitas into strips, place on a baking sheet and bake in a preheated 400°F/200°C oven for about 8 minutes, or until golden and crunchy.)
5. Just before serving, add lettuce to tomatoes and toss gently.
6. Shape two strips of cucumber (overlapping ends of strips) into a ring about 8 inches (20 cm) in diameter and place on individual serving plates.
7. Fill cucumber rings with salad. Place wedges or strips of grilled pita across each serving.

MAKES 6 TO 8 SERVINGS

Swordfish Souvlaki with Lemon Dressing

You can also make these using 1-inch (2.5 cm) chunks of extra-firm tofu, lamb, chicken or fresh tuna (grill the tuna just until rare).

Serve the souvlaki drizzled with the lemon dressing and with tzatziki, if you wish.

2 lb (1 kg) boneless, skinless swordfish, cut in 1-inch (2.5 cm) cubes
¼ cup (50 mL) extra-virgin olive oil
1 tsp (5 mL) kosher salt
½ tsp (2 mL) pepper
1 tbsp (15 mL) grated lemon peel
1 tbsp (15 mL) chopped fresh oregano, or 1 tsp (5 mL) dried
2 cloves garlic, minced

LEMON DRESSING
3 tbsp (45 mL) lemon juice
1 tsp (5 mL) kosher salt
¼ tsp (1 mL) pepper
⅓ cup (75 mL) extra-virgin olive oil
1 tbsp (15 mL) chopped fresh oregano or thyme, or 1 tsp (5 mL) dried

½ cup (125 mL) pitted black olives
1 cup (250 mL) cherry tomatoes, halved if large
12 sprigs fresh parsley
1 lemon, sliced or cut in wedges

1. In a large bowl, combine fish, oil, salt, pepper, lemon peel, oregano and garlic. Toss together well and marinate for 10 minutes.
2. To prepare dressing, in a separate bowl, combine lemon juice, salt, pepper, oil and oregano.
3. Thread 3 or 4 pieces of fish on each skewer (preferably metal). Grill for 2 to 3 minutes per side (about 8 to 10 minutes in total).
4. Serve fish topped with olives and tomatoes and drizzle with dressing. Garnish with parsley and lemon.

MAKES 6 TO 8 SERVINGS

Tzatziki

In a food processor or blender, combine 2 peeled garlic cloves, 1 tbsp (15 mL) lemon juice, 1 cup (250 mL) yogurt cheese or thick unflavored yogurt, 2 tbsp (25 mL) tahina, 1 tsp (5 mL) kosher salt, 2 tbsp (25 mL) chopped fresh dill or mint and ¼ tsp (1 mL) hot red pepper sauce. Process until smooth. Taste and adjust seasonings if necessary.

Makes about 1 cup (250 mL).

Yogurt Cheese

Place 3 cups (750 mL) unflavored yogurt in a strainer lined with cheesecloth, paper towel or coffee filter. Place over a bowl. Refrigerate for a few hours or overnight (the longer it drains, the thicker it becomes). Discard drained liquid (or use in baking) and refrigerate yogurt cheese.

Makes about 1½ cups (375 mL).

Mediterranean Rice Pilaf

This rice pilaf is delicious any time, but it is really perfect served with the swordfish souvlaki or with a Middle Eastern tagine (pages 66–69). If you want to use brown rice, use 4 cups / 1 L liquid and cook for 30 to 40 minutes.

3 tbsp (45 mL) extra-virgin olive oil or butter
2 onions, sliced
½ cup (125 mL) broken vermicelli pasta
2 cups (500 mL) long-grain rice (preferably basmati), well rinsed and drained
3½ cups (875 mL) chicken stock or water
2 tsp (10 mL) kosher salt
¼ tsp (1 mL) pepper
2 tbsp (25 mL) chopped preserved lemon peel,
   or 1 tbsp (15 mL) grated lemon peel

1. Heat oil in a large saucepan or Dutch oven over medium heat. Add onions and cook gently for 10 to 15 minutes, or until browned.
2. Add noodles and cook for a few minutes until pasta begins to brown. Add rice and coat well with onion mixture.
3. Add stock and bring to a boil. Stir in salt, pepper and lemon. Reduce heat, cover and cook for 15 minutes, or until stock is absorbed and rice is tender. Remove from heat and keep covered until ready to serve.

MAKES 6 TO 8 SERVINGS

Greek Wedding Cookies

Tender and delicate, these cookies really melt in your mouth. They freeze well, but are very fragile.

1 cup (250 mL) butter
¼ cup (50 mL) granulated sugar
1 egg yolk
2 tsp (10 mL) vanilla paste or pure vanilla extract
2 cups (500 mL) all-purpose flour
1 ½ cups (375 mL) finely chopped pecans
Icing sugar, sifted

1. In a large bowl, beat butter until light. Beat in sugar.
2. Beat in egg yolk and vanilla. Stir in flour just until combined. Stir in pecans. Refrigerate dough for 2 hours or overnight.
3. Shape dough into 1-inch (2.5 cm) balls. Place on parchment-lined baking sheets.
4. Bake in a preheated 325°F (160°C) oven for 25 minutes, or until cookies are just starting to turn brown. Cool on baking sheet for 5 minutes before transferring to a rack. Sift icing sugar heavily over top of cookies while still warm and again when cool.

MAKES ABOUT 60 COOKIES

Lemon Yogurt Cake with Lemon Glaze

This is one of our favorite cakes, and we make it all the time. We have baked it in Bundt pans, tube pans, loaf pans and round cake pans, and it is always delicious, though the baking time may vary depending on which pan you use. Use a cake tester or bake until a meat thermometer registers 185°F (85°C). This cake is perfect plain, or served with mixed berries, lemon curd (page 129) or caramel sauce (page 43).

¾ cup (175 mL) butter
1 cup (250 mL) granulated sugar
2 eggs
1 tsp (5 mL) vanilla paste or pure vanilla extract
2 tbsp (25 mL) grated lemon peel
1¾ cups (425 mL) all-purpose flour
2 tsp (10 mL) baking powder
1 tsp (5 mL) baking soda
Pinch kosher salt
1 cup (250 mL) unflavored yogurt or buttermilk

LEMON GLAZE
2 tbsp (25 mL) lemon juice
1 cup (250 mL) sifted icing sugar

1. In a large bowl, cream butter and granulated sugar. Beat in eggs one at a time. Beat in vanilla and lemon peel.
2. In a separate bowl, combine flour, baking powder, baking soda and salt.
3. Add flour to butter mixture alternately with yogurt in 3 or 4 additions, beginning and ending with flour. After each addition, stir just until combined.
4. Spoon batter into a parchment-lined 9- x 5-inch (2 L) loaf pan. Bake in a preheated 350°F (180°) oven for 40 to 45 minutes, or until a toothpick or cake tester inserted in cake comes out clean.
5. Cool cake in pan for 10 minutes. Loosen cake around edges, remove from pan and transfer to a rack.
6. Meanwhile, combine lemon juice and icing sugar. Mixture should be runny. When cake is cool, drizzle glaze over cake.

MAKES ONE LOAF CAKE

Mixed Berry Salad

In a bowl, combine 2 cups (500 mL) fresh strawberries and 2 tbsp (25 mL) granulated sugar. Let stand at room temperature for 30 minutes.

Gently stir in 1 cup (250 mL) fresh raspberries and 1 cup (250 mL) fresh blueberries or blackberries.

Makes about 4 cups (1 L).

MARGARITA MARTINIS

UNSANDWICHES (LETTUCE ROLLUPS)

GRILLED LAMB WITH PRESERVED LEMONS AND SHALLOTS

ROASTED SWEET POTATOES WITH SWEET CHILI SAUCE AND LIME

ARUGULA AND ALMOND SALAD WITH

PRESERVED LEMON DRESSING

PECAN PIE SQUARES WITH CHOCOLATE

australian dinner

SERVES 8

Ray and I recently visited Australia for a global food media event called Tasting Australia. We ate wonderful meals at beautiful venues, from wineries to beaches. We were served lettuce rollups at one of many standing-up dinners and a lamb dish similar to the one in this menu was prepared at a cooking class at the stunning Chapel Hill Winery in the McLaren Vale wine region of South Australia.

Marinate the lamb and prepare the dessert, drinks, salad dressing and appetizers ahead. Cook the lamb and toss the salad just before serving (the sweet potatoes can be prepared ahead, or they can be roasted in the oven alongside the lamb). I serve the salad on top of the lamb, the way they did in Australia, but you can serve it alongside or afterwards if you wish.

Margarita Martinis

I like to serve this on ice. The ice waters down the drink a little, which is a good thing for me, though most people can handle it straight up. You can also make a pitcher and refrigerate until ready to serve.

> 3 tbsp (45 mL) tequila
> 1 tbsp (15 mL) orange liqueur
> 3 tbsp (45 mL) lime juice (plus a little extra for moistening rim of glass)
> 2 tbsp (25 mL) sugar syrup (page 86) or granulated sugar
> ¼ cup (50 mL) kosher salt

1. Combine tequila, liqueur, lime juice and sugar syrup in a cocktail shaker. Add a handful of ice cubes. Shake about 10 times, or until shaker is too cold to handle.
2. Spread salt on a small plate. Moisten rim of a martini glass with lime juice or rub a piece of lime around the rim. Dip rim into salt to create a thin, even crust all around rim. Strain martini into glass.

MAKES 1 DRINK

Unsandwiches (Lettuce Rollups)

We had these fantastic appetizers at an Australian winery where we were served buffet style and ate standing up (see Standing-up menu for more buffet recipes). Larger lettuce leaves have to be rolled up before eating, so to make these easier to handle, I like to use the small inside leaves that look like little cups, or Belgian endive leaves. (You may need a few heads of Boston lettuce, but you can always use the outside leaves in a salad.)

You can also use ground turkey, lamb, beef or diced tofu instead of the chicken. For a nice crunch, sprinkle Rice Krispies and/or toasted pine nuts on top.

2 tbsp (25 mL) soy sauce
2 tbsp (25 mL) oyster sauce
¼ cup (50 mL) water
1 tsp (5 mL) roasted sesame oil
½ tsp (2 mL) granulated sugar
1 tsp (5 mL) cornstarch
1 tbsp (15 mL) extra-virgin olive oil
2 cloves garlic, finely chopped
1 tbsp (15 mL) chopped fresh ginger
½ tsp (2 mL) hot chili paste
1 lb (500 g) ground chicken
½ cup (125 mL) green peas
½ cup (125 mL) diced water chestnuts or jicama
2 green onions, chopped
24 small leaves Boston lettuce or Belgian endive

1. In a small bowl, combine soy sauce, oyster sauce, water, sesame oil, sugar and cornstarch.
2. Heat olive oil in a wok or large skillet over medium-high heat. Add garlic, ginger and chili paste and stir-fry for about 30 seconds, or until fragrant.
3. Add chicken and stir-fry for 4 to 5 minutes, or until brown.
4. Stir cornstarch mixture into chicken and cook for 3 to 4 minutes, or until thick.
5. Add peas and water chestnuts and cook for 1 minute, or until hot. Stir in green onions and cool slightly.
6. Spoon chicken mixture into lettuce cups.

MAKES 24 APPETIZERS

Grilled Lamb with Preserved Lemons and Shallots

I love serving butterflied leg of lamb. It is boned out and somewhat flat, so it cooks quickly but, because it is not completely even, some parts are more well done and some are rarer, pleasing everyone. I like my lamb medium-rare, and always use a meat thermometer to be sure.

Preserved lemons have a delicious, unique flavor. Buy them in Middle Eastern stores or, better yet, make your own (page 69).

You can cook the lamb entirely on the grill for about 10 to 15 minutes per side, but I like to brown it on the grill and then finish it in the oven.

1 5-lb (2.5 kg) butterflied leg of lamb, trimmed
1 tbsp (15 mL) paprika (preferably smoked)
1 tbsp (15 mL) kosher salt
Peel of 1 preserved lemon, rinsed and very thinly sliced,
    or 1 tbsp (15 mL) grated lemon peel
8 shallots or 2 onions, very thinly sliced
2 tbsp (25 mL) finely chopped fresh rosemary
¼ tsp (1 mL) hot red pepper flakes
¼ cup (50 mL) extra-virgin olive oil

1. Flatten lamb as much as possible. Place in a large dish.
2. In a small bowl, combine paprika, salt, lemon, shallots, rosemary, hot pepper flakes and oil. Pour over lamb and rub in. Marinate for 1 hour at room temperature or for a few hours in refrigerator.
3. Grill lamb for 5 minutes per side. Transfer to a baking sheet.
4. Roast lamb in a preheated 400°F (200°C) oven for 15 to 20 minutes or longer (until a meat thermometer reaches 135°F/57°C for medium-rare). Remove lamb to a carving board, cover loosely with foil and let rest for 10 minutes before carving.

MAKES 8 SERVINGS

Roasted Sweet Potatoes with Sweet Chili Sauce and Lime

You can also use butternut or buttercup squash in this recipe. The sauce can be used on fish or chicken or served as a dip for satays, dumplings or spring rolls.

3 lb (1.5 kg) sweet potatoes, peeled and cut in slices ½ inch (1 cm) thick
3 tbsp (45 mL) extra-virgin olive oil
1 ½ tsp (7 mL) kosher salt

SWEET CHILI SAUCE
¼ cup (50 mL) sweet Thai chili sauce or hot red pepper jelly
1 tbsp (15 mL) lime juice
1 tbsp (15 mL) seasoned rice vinegar
1 clove garlic, minced
¼ tsp (1 mL) roasted sesame oil
2 tbsp (25 mL) chopped fresh cilantro

1. In a large bowl, toss sweet potatoes with olive oil and salt. Spread in a single layer on a parchment-lined baking sheet. Roast in a preheated 400°F (200°C) oven for 30 to 40 minutes, or until tender.
2. Meanwhile, in a small bowl, combine sweet chili sauce, lime juice, vinegar, garlic, sesame oil and cilantro.
3. Spoon dressing over sweet potatoes and toss gently. Serve hot or at room temperature.

MAKES 8 SERVINGS

Arugula and Almond Salad with Preserved Lemon Dressing

This salad is great with lamb or as part of any Middle Eastern or Mediterranean meal. The dressing, from Toronto chef Ezra Title, is wonderful on any green salad.

PRESERVED LEMON DRESSING
2 tbsp (25 mL) chopped preserved lemon peel,
    or 1 tbsp (15 mL) grated lemon peel
2 tbsp (25 mL) lemon juice
½ tsp (2 mL) granulated sugar
½ cup (125 mL) extra-virgin olive oil
½ tsp (2 mL) kosher salt
Pinch pepper

SALAD
12 cups (3 L) baby arugula or mixed salad greens
¼ cup (50 mL) fresh cilantro
¼ cup (50 mL) coarsely chopped fresh parsley
3 green onions, thinly sliced
½ cup (125 mL) coarsely chopped toasted almonds

1. To prepare dressing, in a food processor, combine preserved lemon, lemon juice and sugar. Add oil slowly to create an emulsion. Season with salt and pepper.
2. In a bowl, combine arugula, cilantro, parsley and green onions. Toss with as much dressing as you need. Sprinkle with almonds.

MAKES 8 TO 10 SERVINGS

Pecan Pie Squares with Chocolate

Turning pecan pie into pecan pie squares is a great idea from Chicago restaurateur and cookbook author Rick Bayless. You can also cut smaller squares to serve as cookies or little treats.

1½ cups (375 mL) all-purpose flour
¼ tsp (1 mL) kosher salt
¾ cup (175 mL) butter or margarine, cold, cut in small pieces

FILLING
2 cups (500 mL) pecan halves, toasted and coarsely chopped
1 cup (250 mL) chopped semisweet or bittersweet chocolate (about 8 oz / 250 g)
½ cup (125 mL) butter or margarine
1 cup (250 mL) packed brown sugar
5 eggs
¾ cup (175 mL) corn syrup
¼ cup (50 mL) molasses
2 tsp (10 mL) vanilla paste or pure vanilla extract
3 tbsp (45 mL) all-purpose flour

1. Combine flour and salt in a food processor. Add butter and process on/off until it is in tiny bits and dough is just starting to come together.
2. Pat dough into bottom of a 13- x 9-inch (3 L) oiled and parchment-lined baking dish.
3. Bake crust in a preheated 350°F (180°C) oven for 20 to 25 minutes, or until lightly browned. Cool for 30 minutes at room temperature. Sprinkle with pecans and chocolate.
4. In a food processor, cream butter and brown sugar for 3 minutes. Beat in eggs one at a time. Beat in corn syrup, molasses, flour and vanilla. Pour over pecans and chocolate.
5. Spread filling over baked crust and bake for 30 to 35 minutes, or until a knife inserted into center comes out clean. Cool for 1 hour before cutting into squares.

MAKES 12 LARGE SQUARES

graduation dinner

SERVES 6 TO 8

When Anna graduated from Huron College at the University of Western Ontario, we really had a wonderful day. It was like being in a Harry Potter movie—the processions, the banners, the regalia—everything was magical. The Friday night after her grad we had a celebration dinner, and of course I cooked some of her favorite foods.

Except for the final grilling of the chicken and ribs and the tossing of the salad, this entire menu can be prepared ahead. Marinate the chicken and ribs in the refrigerator overnight.

Green Goddess Garden Shooters

I don't normally like things that are too cutesy, but these are so adorable that I can't resist. Guests have their own mini containers and can double dip as much as they like!

I like these served with all green vegetables, but you could add carrot sticks, fennel, red pepper strips or other vegetables. Of course, if you don't have shooter glasses, you can always serve this in a bowl surrounded by veggies like a regular dip.

The dip is also delicious as a drizzle on asparagus, as a salad dressing, sandwich spread or topping for burgers.

    1 clove garlic, peeled
    2 anchovies, rinsed, or 1 tbsp (15 mL) anchovy paste
    2 green onions, chopped
    2 tbsp (25 mL) chopped fresh tarragon, or ½ tsp (2 mL) dried
    2 tbsp (25 mL) chopped fresh parsley
    2 tbsp (25 mL) chopped fresh cilantro
    ¾ cup (175 mL) mayonnaise
    ¾ cup (175 mL) sour cream or soy sour cream
    ½ ripe avocado
    2 tbsp (25 mL) lemon juice
    Salt and pepper to taste
    4 Belgian endives, separated and halved lengthwise
    8 oz (250 g) green beans, trimmed and blanched
    1 lb (500 g) thin asparagus, trimmed and blanched

1. In a food processor, chop garlic, anchovies, green onions, tarragon, parsley and cilantro.
2. Add mayonnaise, sour cream, avocado and lemon juice. Puree. Season with salt and pepper.
3. Place dip in 6 to 8 shooter glasses (about 2 to 3 tbsp/25 to 45 mL per glass) and arrange Belgian endives, green beans and asparagus spears standing up in dip.

MAKES ABOUT 2 CUPS (500 ML) DIP

North African Spiced Chicken Skewers

We developed this recipe for our book club when we featured Carol Off's *Bitter Chocolate*—an investigative report on the chocolate industry. We included chocolate in every course. These chicken skewers were so popular that I have made them over and over, in classes and at home. We always grill the chicken breasts or thighs whole and then cut them up and skewer them to serve so the bamboo skewers won't burn up on the barbecue.

These are also great drizzled with tahina (page 194).

1 tbsp (15 mL) cocoa powder

1 tsp (5 mL) ground cumin

2 tbsp (25 mL) brown sugar

2 tsp (10 mL) kosher salt

¼ tsp (1 mL) ground cinnamon

¼ tsp (1 mL) ground allspice

1 tsp (5 mL) harissa, ½ tsp (2 mL) hot red pepper flakes or aleppo pepper, or more to taste

2 cloves garlic, minced

⅓ cup (75 mL) extra-virgin olive oil

2 lb (1 kg) boneless, skinless chicken breasts or thighs

1. In a small bowl, combine cocoa, cumin, sugar, salt, cinnamon, allspice, harissa, garlic and oil.
2. Coat chicken with paste and refrigerate up to overnight.
3. Grill chicken breasts for 5 minutes per side or thighs for 8 to 10 minutes per side, or until just cooked through. Cut into strips and thread on bamboo skewers.

MAKES 24 SKEWERS

Miami Ribs with Pineapple Glaze

When shortribs are sliced really thin (¼ inch / 5 mm thick) and marinated, they can be grilled very quickly (they are usually called Miami ribs). They'll be slightly chewy but tender and flavorful at the same time.

At an event for Second Harvest (Toronto's food recovery program), I tasted Miami ribs made with a pineapple glaze from Flow restaurant. This is my version. The marinade is sweet but the ribs don't burn because they cook so quickly.

These can also be served as an appetizer. Have them sliced extra thin, cook until crisp and cut into individual pieces between the bones.

1 cup (250 mL) pineapple juice
½ cup (125 mL) rice vinegar
⅓ cup (75 mL) soy sauce
2 tbsp (25 mL) Worcestershire sauce
1 tbsp (15 mL) lemon juice
1 tbsp (15 mL) roasted sesame oil
½ tsp (2 mL) hot red pepper sauce
3 cloves garlic, minced
1 tbsp (15 mL) finely chopped fresh ginger
⅓ cup (75 mL) granulated sugar
⅓ cup (75 mL) brown sugar
4 lb (2 kg) Miami shortribs, sliced about ¼ inch (5 mm) thick

1. In a large bowl, combine pineapple juice, vinegar, soy sauce, Worcestershire, lemon juice, sesame oil, hot pepper sauce, garlic, ginger, granulated sugar and brown sugar.
2. Add ribs and turn to coat well. Marinate up to overnight in refrigerator.
3. Drain ribs and grill for 3 to 4 minutes per side, or until well browned and crispy.

MAKES 6 TO 8 SERVINGS

Warm Roasted Potato Salad

Potato salad made with roasted potatoes is so good that you may never boil potatoes for salad again. Toss the potatoes with the dressing as soon as they come out of the oven. You can turn this into a Niçoise potato salad by adding cherry tomatoes, green beans, black olives, hard-cooked eggs and chunks of tuna.

   Serve this warm or at room temperature, but don't refrigerate it.

3 lb (1.5 kg) small Yukon gold potatoes or red potatoes, cut in half if large
2 tbsp (25 mL) extra-virgin olive oil
2 tsp (10 mL) kosher salt

DRESSING
1 tbsp (15 mL) sherry vinegar
2 cloves garlic, minced
½ tsp (2 mL) kosher salt
1 tbsp (15 mL) grainy mustard
¼ cup (50 mL) extra-virgin olive oil
2 tbsp (25 mL) chopped fresh parsley
4 cups (1 L) baby arugula

1. In a large bowl, toss potatoes with oil and salt. Spread in a single layer on a parchment-lined baking sheet and roast in a preheated 425°F (220°C) oven for 40 to 45 minutes, or until browned, crisp and tender.
2. Meanwhile, to prepare dressing, in a large bowl, combine vinegar, garlic, salt and mustard. Whisk in oil. Stir in parsley.
3. Add hot potatoes to dressing and toss. Serve warm or at room temperature on a bed of arugula.

MAKES 6 TO 8 SERVINGS

Mexican Grilled Corn Salad

This salad is always a big hit. I got the idea from Anna's best friend, Julia Sharp. She reminded me of a delicious corn dish I first had at the Maxwell Street Market in Chicago, where vendors boil corn on the cob, slather it with mayo, dredge it in Parmesan, sprinkle it with cumin and chili powder and then drizzle it with a little lime juice. I converted that idea into this amazing salad for easy summer entertaining. You can also boil the corn instead of grilling it.

  8 ears corn, husked
  ½ cup (125 mL) mayonnaise
  1 clove garlic, minced
  3 tbsp (45 mL) lime juice
  1 tsp (5 mL) ground cumin
  ½ tsp (2 mL) hot red pepper sauce
  2 tbsp (25 mL) chopped fresh cilantro
  ¼ cup (50 mL) grated Parmesan cheese, optional
  Salt and pepper to taste

1. Grill corn, turning every minute or two, until dotted with brown on all sides. Cool. Cut cobs in half. Place cut side down on a cutting board and slice off kernels. Place corn in a bowl.
2. In a separate bowl, combine mayonnaise, garlic, lime juice, cumin, hot pepper sauce, cilantro and cheese, if using. Season with salt and pepper to taste.
3. Toss corn with dressing.

MAKES 6 TO 8 SERVINGS

Grilled Corn on the Cob
Grilling corn directly on the barbecue only takes a few minutes, and you get the real flavor of fire.

Remove husks and silk from 8 ears of corn. Grill corn for 3 to 4 minutes, or until lightly browned on all sides. Serve as is or with this delicious flavored mixture.

In a small bowl, combine 2 tbsp (25 mL) extra-virgin olive oil or butter, 1 minced clove garlic, ½ tsp (2 mL) kosher salt and 2 tbsp (25 mL) shredded fresh basil. Brush lightly over hot corn.

Makes 8 servings.

Tomato and Avocado Salad

When my friend Susan Devins and her family moved to Singapore, there were a lot of goodbye parties. Susan's colleague Elizabeth Pizzinato served a spectacular dinner that included this salad. She said she based it on a Bobby Flay recipe, and I have based mine on hers—salad twice removed.

Cherry tomatoes or campari tomatoes work well when local tomatoes are not the best. Use ripe avocados and fresh lime juice, and toast the cumin seeds for the best flavor.

1 ½ lb (750 g) ripe tomatoes, cut in chunks, or cherry tomatoes
8 cups (2 L) salad greens
2 ripe avocados, cut in chunks
3 tbsp (45 mL) chopped fresh cilantro

LIME CUMIN DRESSING
¼ cup (50 mL) lime juice
1 clove garlic, minced
1 tbsp (15 mL) honey
½ tsp (2 mL) kosher salt
1 tbsp (15 mL) cumin seeds, toasted and lightly crushed,
    or ½ tsp (2 mL) ground cumin
⅓ cup (75 mL) sunflower oil or extra-virgin olive oil

1. In a large bowl, combine tomatoes, greens, avocados and cilantro.
2. To prepare dressing, in a small bowl, combine lime juice, garlic, honey, salt and cumin. Whisk in oil. Taste and adjust seasonings if necessary.
3. Toss salad with dressing to taste.

MAKES 6 TO 8 SERVINGS

Really Easy Chocolate Cupcakes

For Anna's graduation dinner she wanted chocolate cupcakes, but you can also use this batter to make a quick and gorgeous chocolate cake. This recipe is from Mitchell Davis, who got it from his sister Carrie, a great baker.

These cupcakes are moist and delicious on their own, with the non-dairy glaze, or with the ganache. When the ganache is barely warm you can use it as a glaze. When it is thick but spreadable, use it as a great frosting. When it is cold and firm it can be used to make truffles.

1 ¾ cups (425 mL) all-purpose flour

1 cup (250 mL) granulated sugar

1 cup (250 mL) packed brown sugar

¾ cup (175 mL) cocoa powder

2 tsp (10 mL) baking soda

1 tsp (5 mL) baking powder

¼ tsp (1 mL) kosher salt

2 eggs

1 cup (250 mL) strong coffee, cooled

1 cup (250 mL) buttermilk, sour soy milk (page 278),
    sour cream or unflavored yogurt

½ cup (125 mL) vegetable oil

1 tbsp (15 mL) vanilla paste or pure vanilla extract

GANACHE FROSTING (OPTIONAL)

1 ½ cups (375 mL) whipping cream

12 oz (375 g) bittersweet or semisweet chocolate, chopped

1 tsp (5 mL) vanilla paste or pure vanilla extract

1. In a large bowl, sift together flour, granulated sugar, brown sugar, cocoa, baking soda, baking powder and salt.

2. In separate bowl, whisk together eggs, coffee, buttermilk, oil and vanilla.

3. Pour liquid ingredients over dry ingredients and stir together just until mixed.

4. Grease and flour muffin pans or spray with nonstick cooking spray (use 18 regular muffin cups or 44 mini muffin cups). Pour batter into muffin cups and bake larger cupcakes in a preheated 350°F (180°C) oven for 20 minutes and mini cupcakes for 12 minutes. Cool completely.

5. Meanwhile, if you are making ganache, heat whipping cream in a microwave or in a saucepan. It should just start to bubble and be quite hot. (Be careful, as it can boil over easily.)

6. Place chopped chocolate in a heatproof bowl and pour cream over chocolate. Shake bowl a bit so chocolate is covered with cream. Cover and let sit for 10 minutes. Stir. Chocolate should melt completely and be very smooth. Stir in vanilla. (If there are still pieces of chocolate, heat gently until melted.) Cool mixture, stirring occasionally, until spreadable. If you want to cool it faster, place bowl in a larger bowl of ice and water. This will cause the chocolate to thicken quickly so be sure to stir every few minutes so you know when it is perfect.

7. Swirl or pipe frosting over cooled cupcakes.

MAKES 18 REGULAR CUPCAKES OR 44 MINI CUPCAKES

Really Easy Chocolate Cake

Divide batter between two 9-inch (23 cm) cake pans that have been greased and lined with a circle of parchment paper. Bake in a preheated 350°F (180°C) oven 25 to 30 minutes, or until center springs back when lightly touched, sides of cake pull away from pan and a cake tester comes out clean.

Cool on a rack for 10 minutes. Run a knife around edge of cake and invert on a rack. Cool completely before icing.

Non-dairy Chocolate Glaze

In a saucepan, combine 1 cup (250 mL) granulated sugar and 1 ½ cups (375 mL) coffee, water or wine. Bring to a boil and stir to dissolve sugar. Reduce heat and cook gently for a few minutes. Remove from heat and add 1 lb (500 g) chopped bittersweet or semi-sweet chocolate. Stir until smooth. Stir in 2 tsp (10 mL) vanilla paste or pure vanilla extract. Cool. (If sauce becomes too thick as it cools, warm slightly before using.)

MINI GOUGÈRES WITH CREAMY SCRAMBLED EGGS
OR
CHICKEN SKEWERS GLAZED WITH POMEGRANATE MOLASSES
BREADED CHICKEN CUTLETS
ROASTED ASPARAGUS
ROASTED ROOT VEGETABLE "FRIES"
NO-KNEAD ARTISANAL BREAD
CHERRY BERRY LATTICE TART
AUNT REBA'S OATMEAL COOKIES

dinner with the kids

SERVES 6

Some of my favorite dinners happen when my kids invite their friends over. They are so bright and fresh with their futures all ahead of them—it is glorious to see. There is lots of talking and laughing around the table, and it is so lively. I love having a full house—I am one mother who hates being an empty nester, and after four years I'm still not used to it.

Here's a meal they all went crazy over. (I don't usually serve two chicken dishes in the same menu, but sometimes it is the only meat kids will eat.)

You can marinate the chicken skewers, bread the chicken for the main course, make the tartar sauce and bake the gougères, bread and dessert ahead of time.

Mini Gougères with Creamy Scrambled Eggs

Gougère is the savory version of the pastry (patachou)—used to make cream puffs, éclairs, gâteau St. Honoré, etc. It is easy to make and very delicious.

Serve these on their own or filled with scrambled eggs or creamy goat cheese (sometimes I add a thin slice of smoked salmon). Blue cheese or Brie with caramelized onions (page 287) or smoked Cheddar with red pepper jelly also make great filling combinations (I use Lappi cheese for my lactose-intolerant bunch).

 1 cup (250 mL) water
 ⅓ cup (75 mL) butter, cut in small pieces, or extra-virgin olive oil
 1 cup (250 mL) all-purpose flour
 4 eggs
 1½ tsp (7 mL) kosher salt
 1 tbsp (15 mL) pepper
 1 tsp (5 mL) Dijon mustard
 1½ cups (375 mL) grated Gruyère cheese, optional

 FILLING
 Creamy Scrambled Eggs

1. Place water and butter in a medium saucepan and bring to a boil. Remove from heat and stir in flour all at once. Keep stirring until dough comes away from sides of pan and forms a ball.

2. Return pan to heat and cook gently over medium heat for 2 to 3 minutes, stirring constantly, until dough dries out a bit and leaves a thin film on bottom of pan. Transfer dough to a large bowl and cool for 5 minutes.

3. With a wooden spoon or electric mixer, beat in eggs one at a time. Dough will squish around and then come together and that's when you add the next egg.

4. Beat in salt, pepper, mustard and Gruyère, if using.

5. Drop dough by 1½ tbsp (22 mL) onto a parchment-lined baking sheet. Bake in a preheated 425°F (220°C) oven for 25 to 30 minutes, or until pastries are puffed and browned.

6. Let pastries cool. Cut each gougère in half and fill with scrambled eggs.

MAKES ABOUT 36

Creamy Scrambled Eggs

Ezra Title is a Toronto chef and caterer who makes wonderful breakfasts at the Brick Works Market every Saturday morning. He says the secret to traditional French-style scrambled eggs is to take your time and cook them over very gentle heat so they don't become too firm.

In a bowl, whisk together 4 eggs.

Heat 1 tbsp (15 mL) extra-virgin olive oil in a large skillet over medium-low heat. Add eggs and a pinch of salt (sometimes I use truffle salt if I am cooking for adults) and pepper. Using a whisk, stir eggs for 3 to 5 minutes, or until creamy.

Remove eggs from heat. Using a rubber spatula, stir in 1 tbsp (15 mL) butter or margarine and 1 tbsp (15 mL) milk or soy milk. Taste and adjust seasonings if necessary. Stir in 1 tbsp (15 mL) chopped chives.

Chicken Skewers Glazed with Pomegranate Molasses

Kids of all ages love food on skewers. Serve these as appetizers on skewers or leave the chicken breasts whole and serve as a main course with rice pilaf.

¼ cup (50 mL) pomegranate molasses
3 tbsp (45 mL) lime juice
3 tbsp (45 mL) extra-virgin olive oil
2 cloves garlic, minced
1 tbsp (15 mL) sweet Thai chili sauce, or 1 tsp (5 mL) hot chili paste
1 tsp (5 mL) kosher salt
2 lb (1 kg) boneless, skinless chicken breasts

1. In a small bowl, combine pomegranate molasses, lime juice, oil, garlic, chili sauce and salt.
2. Remove filets from chicken breasts and pour marinade over filets and large chicken pieces. Coat well. Refrigerate until ready to cook.
3. Grill chicken breasts for about 4 to 5 minutes per side, or until chicken is just cooked or reaches 165°F (75°C) on a meat thermometer. Grill filets for about 2 minutes per side.
4. Cut large chicken pieces crosswise into fingers and thread onto bamboo skewers. Skewer the little filets whole.

MAKES 24 SKEWERS

Breaded Chicken Cutlets

Everyone loves breaded foods. Use this basic recipe to make breaded fish or veal cutlets, or cut fish or chicken into strips and make fish or chicken fingers. Serve the cutlets plain or with tartare sauce (usually reserved for fish but great on chicken too).

If you don't want to fry the chicken, place it in a single layer on wire rack placed on a baking sheet. Drizzle the cutlets with oil and bake at 400°F (200°C) for 20 to 25 minutes.

> 2 lb (1 kg) boneless, skinless chicken breasts
> 1 tsp (5 mL) kosher salt
> 1 cup (250 mL) all-purpose flour
> 3 eggs
> 2 cups (500 mL) panko or fresh breadcrumbs
> ¼ cup (50 mL) vegetable oil, or more if necessary
> 1 tbsp (15 mL) lemon juice, optional
> 2 tbsp (25 mL) butter, optional

1. Remove filets from chicken and pound chicken breasts until flat. Pat chicken dry and sprinkle with salt.
2. Place flour in a shallow dish. Beat eggs in another shallow dish. Place breadcrumbs in a third shallow dish. Dip chicken breasts and filets into flour and shake off excess. Dip into eggs and allow excess to drip off. Lay chicken in breadcrumbs and pat crumbs in firmly. Arrange chicken on a rack set over a baking sheet to dry. If not cooking right away, refrigerate.
3. To cook, heat oil in a large skillet over medium-high heat. Cook chicken, in batches, for 2 to 3 minutes per side, or until browned. Drain on paper towels.
4. Wipe out pan. Add lemon juice and butter, if using. When butter melts, drizzle over chicken.

MAKES 6 SERVINGS

Tartare Sauce

In a bowl, combine ½ cup (125 mL) mayonnaise, 2 tbsp (25 mL) chopped gherkins or dill pickle, 1 tbsp (15 mL) lemon juice, 1 tsp (5 mL) grainy or Dijon mustard, 1 tbsp (15 mL) finely chopped shallots, chives or green onions, 1 tbsp (15 mL) chopped fresh tarragon and 1 tbsp (15 mL) chopped fresh parsley.

Makes about ¾ cup (175 mL).

Roasted Asparagus

Here is an easy and delicious way to cook asparagus. Roasting concentrates the flavors.

2 lb (1 kg) asparagus
2 tbsp (25 mL) extra-virgin olive oil
½ tsp (2 mL) kosher salt

1. Trim about 1 inch (2.5 cm) off base of asparagus stalks. If stalks are thick, peel about 1 inch (2.5 cm) from bottom of stalks.
2. Spread asparagus on a parchment-lined baking sheet and toss with oil and salt. Roast in a preheated 400°F (200°C) oven for 10 to 15 minutes, or until lightly browned.

MAKES 6 TO 8 SERVINGS

Roasted Root Vegetable "Fries"

I have come to love roasted "fries" even more than regular fries. Use all the veggies or just more of the ones you like.

3 lb (1.5 kg) combination of potatoes, carrots, parsnips and sweet potatoes
3 tbsp (45 mL) extra-virgin olive oil
2 tsp (10 mL) kosher salt
¼ tsp (1 mL) pepper
2 tbsp (25 mL) fresh thyme, or ½ tsp (2 mL) dried
2 tbsp (25 mL) chopped fresh parsley

1. Peel vegetables and cut into sticks about ½ inch (1 cm) thick.
2. In a large bowl, toss vegetables with oil, salt, pepper and thyme. Spread on one or two parchment-lined baking sheets and roast in a preheated 425°F (220°C) oven for 40 to 50 minutes, or until vegetables are browned and tender, turning halfway through cooking time.
3. Toss with parsley.

MAKES 6 TO 8 SERVINGS

No-Knead Artisanal Bread

This bread is so much fun to make. Although I have been baking bread for years, last year I became totally obsessed with this new technique from Jim Lahey of the Sullivan Street Bakery in New York. I had seen Mark Bittman's article about it in the *New York Times*, but it was Cary List, a corporate client with impeccable taste, who told me that I had to try it right away.

It is delicious and easy. It allows you to produce artisanal bread without a special oven—all you need is a heavy, medium-sized cast-iron pot with a lid.

I love this plain or made with two parts all-purpose flour and one part whole wheat. Ray loves it with 1 cup (250 mL) pitted black olives, 1 tbsp (15 mL) chopped fresh rosemary and 1 tbsp (15 mL) coarsely ground black pepper. Fara loves it with ¾ cup (175 mL) each chopped toasted walnuts and golden raisins. Anna loves it with ¾ cup (175 mL) each coarsely chopped dark chocolate and dried cherries, and Mark loves it with 1 cup (250 mL) golden raisins and 1 tbsp (15 mL) lightly crushed fennel seeds. (Sprinkle on the additions just before the last rising when you pat the dough out, and then fold everything in.)

> 3 cups (750 mL) all-purpose flour (or part whole wheat)
> 1 tbsp (15 mL) kosher salt
> ½ tsp (2 mL) dry yeast
> 1½ cups (375 mL) water (plus 1 tbsp/ 15 mL), at room temperature
> Extra flour, wheat bran, cornmeal, sesame seeds, etc.

1. In a large bowl, combine flour, salt and yeast. Stir in water. Dough will be a sticky mess. Cover with plastic wrap. Cover with a tea towel. Let sit at room temperature for 12 to 24 hours. Dough should double and have bubbles on the surface.

2. Lay a clean tea towel on counter and flour heavily. Scoop out dough (it is a little messy) and pat into a rough rectangle. Cover lightly with plastic wrap and let sit for 15 minutes.

3. Place another clean tea towel on work surface. Rub with flour and sprinkle with bran, cornmeal or sesame seeds. (Use enough flour so dough does not stick.) Fold dough into thirds and brush off any extra flour. Fold into thirds again to form a rough cube. Place seam side down on second tea towel and dust top with flour, bran, cornmeal or sesame seeds. Fold tea towel over top. Let rise for 2 hours.

4. After 1½ hours, preheat oven to 450°F (225°C). Place a medium-sized heavy cast-iron pot with a lid (I like Le Creuset, and, yes, the pot goes into the oven empty and covered) in oven and heat for 30 minutes.

5. Very gently slide your hand under tea towel holding bread. Open tea towel (over a tray to catch excess flour). Carefully flip bread into hot pot. Cover and bake at 450°F (225°C) for 30 minutes. Remove lid and bake for 20 to 30 minutes longer, or until browned. Cool on a rack. Be really careful. Pot and bread are extremely hot!

MAKES ONE 9-INCH (23 CM) LOAF

Cherry Berry Lattice Pie

Anna loves cherry pie, and so will you. You can make it with all cherries, blueberries, raspberries, etc., but we like a blend. If you have sour cherries all the better, but use a little more sugar. You can also use peaches, nectarines or plums (no need to peel) or pears or apples (I like to peel those).

If you do not have a cherry pitter, place the cherries on a cutting board, hit them very gently with the side of a chef's knife and remove the pits. Cherry juice often sprays all over (until you get the "gently" part down), so wear black or red.

> 1 recipe All-purpose Pastry (page 43)
> 8 cups (2 L) combination of pitted cherries, blueberries and raspberries
> ½ cup (125 mL) granulated sugar
> ⅓ cup (75 mL) all-purpose flour
> 2 tbsp (25 mL) butter or margarine, cut in bits
> 1 egg, beaten
> ¼ cup (50 mL) coarse sugar

1. Divide dough into two pieces (one should be larger than the other—two-thirds and one-third). Roll larger piece of dough into a 16-inch (40 cm) circle and fit into bottom of a 9-inch (23 cm) pie dish. Trim all but 1-inch (2.5 cm) overhang. Roll out second ball of dough and cut into plain or fluted strips ¾ inch (2 cm) wide.
2. To prepare filling, in a large bowl, combine fruit, granulated sugar, flour and butter. Gently spoon into crust.
3. If you don't want to weave a traditional lattice topping, try this simple version. Arrange 4 or 5 strips of dough over filling, leaving about ¾ inch (2 cm) between each strip. Arrange remaining 4 or 5 strips on diagonal across first strips. Roll overhanging edge of bottom crust over strips to secure them, and crimp edges. Place pie on a baking sheet to catch any drips.
4. Brush lattice with egg and sprinkle with coarse sugar. Bake in a preheated 425°F (220°C) oven for 20 minutes. Reduce heat to 375°F (190°C) and bake for 30 minutes longer, or until pie is well cooked and filling is bubbling. If crust gets too brown, reduce oven temperature and cover pie loosely with foil. Cool on a rack.

MAKES ONE 9-INCH (23 CM) PIE

Aunt Reba's Oatmeal Cookies

These are the best oatmeal cookies ever. My aunt Reba used to bake them for every family gathering.

1 cup (250 mL) butter or margarine
½ cup (125 mL) granulated sugar
¾ cup (175 mL) packed brown sugar
1 egg
½ tsp (2 mL) vanilla paste or pure vanilla extract
½ tsp (2 mL) pure almond extract
1½ cups (375 mL) all-purpose flour
1 tsp (5 mL) baking soda
½ tsp (2 mL) kosher salt
2 cups (500 mL) rolled oats
½ cup (125 mL) finely chopped toasted walnuts, optional

1. In a large bowl, cream butter with both sugars. Beat in egg, vanilla and almond extract.
2. In a separate bowl, combine flour, baking soda and salt.
3. Add flour mixture to large bowl and stir in. Stir in oats and walnuts, if using.
4. Roll dough into small balls, about 1 tbsp (15 mL) each. Place balls on parchment-lined baking sheets and press very flat with a fork or flat bottom of a glass dipped in flour.
5. Bake in a preheated 350°F (180°C) oven for 8 to 12 minutes (these are delicious when slightly underbaked and still chewy, but Aunt Reba liked them crisp, and therefore so do I). Cool on wire racks.

MAKES ABOUT 60 COOKIES

Toasting Nuts
Double the flavor of nuts by toasting them before using. Spread nuts on a baking sheet in a single layer and toast in a preheated 350°F (180°C) oven for 5 to 10 minutes, or until lightly colored. Cool before chopping.

LIME MARTINIS WITH MINT AND GINGER
HUGH CARPENTER'S GRILLED TUNA SKEWERS
OR
SMOKED SALMON CRÊPES WITH HONEY MUSTARD MAYO
BARBECUED CHICKEN WITH LEMON CHIPOTLE BASTE
COLESLAW
MOROCCAN SWEET PEPPER AND BREAD SALAD
SWEET CORNBREAD
BLUEBERRY COBBLER

barbecue dinner

SERVES 8

In the summer we often barbecue on Friday nights. I try to make it as easy on Ray as I can, as he is a great barbecuer if I am a great organizer. One of the kids is usually the runner. He needs a drink, a plate to put the cooked food on, an appetizer, a timer, a fork and knife (for emergency hunger fits), a few pairs of tongs, a meat thermometer, instructions and sometimes even a book to read. Sound familiar? I used to feel bad that he was all alone out there, until I realized that's probably where those guys want to be!

Adding the sparkling wine to the sangria and barbecuing the main course are last-minute affairs, but the chicken can be marinated ahead, and everything else can (and should!) be prepared in advance.

Lime Martinis with Mint and Ginger

In hot weather I often serve this as limeade by adding 4 cups (1 L) sparkling water. For a non-alcoholic version, omit the vodka and use a little less sugar syrup.

¾ cup (175 mL) granulated sugar
¾ cup (175 mL) water
1 2-inch (5 cm) piece fresh ginger, sliced
½ cup (125 mL) fresh mint
1 cup (250 mL) lime juice
1 cup (250 mL) vodka
Ice cubes
8 sprigs fresh mint

1. In a saucepan, combine sugar, water, ginger and ½ cup (125 mL) mint. Bring to a boil. Reduce heat and cook gently for about 5 minutes to infuse flavors. Cool and strain.
2. In a pitcher, combine 1 cup (250 mL) mint syrup, lime juice and vodka. Serve over ice and garnish with a sprig of mint.

MAKES 8 SERVINGS

Hugh Carpenter's Grilled Tuna Skewers

Hugh Carpenter is an amazing cookbook author who teaches at my school every year. He always brings new and exciting recipes that we rush to make as soon as he leaves. This is my version of a tuna skewer we all loved. We serve it with preserved lemon mayo, which also tastes great in sandwiches, sushi rolls and with smoked salmon.

These skewers can be prepared ahead and served at room temperature. Arrange them on a serving platter lined with cilantro and top each skewer with a dab of mayo.

Soak the bamboo skewers in water for 30 to 60 minutes before using. (You can soak skewers ahead and keep them in the freezer for future use.)

1 lb (500 mL) tuna steak, 1 inch (2.5 cm) thick
⅓ cup (75 mL) lemon juice
3 tbsp (45 mL) brown sugar
3 tbsp (45 mL) extra-virgin olive oil
1 clove garlic, minced
1 tsp (5 mL) pureed chipotles
½ tsp (2 mL) ground cumin
½ tsp (2 mL) kosher salt
2 tbsp (25 mL) chopped fresh cilantro

PRESERVED LEMON MAYONNAISE
⅓ cup (75 mL) mayonnaise
1 tbsp (15 mL) finely chopped preserved lemon peel,
    or 1 tsp (5 mL) lemon juice

1. Cut tuna into strips about ½ inch (1 cm) thick 2 inches (5 cm) long. Skewer tuna strips lengthwise on bamboo skewers without tips of skewers showing.
2. In a small bowl, combine lemon juice, sugar, oil, garlic, chipotles, cumin, salt and cilantro. Just before grilling, pour marinade over tuna.
3. To prepare mayo, in a small bowl, combine mayonnaise and preserved lemon.
4. Grill tuna for about 30 to 45 seconds per side, or just until seared. Serve with mayo.

MAKES ABOUT 16 SKEWERS

Smoked Salmon Crêpes with Honey Mustard Mayo

These crêpes make a great appetizer, but they can also be served for brunch or lunch.

A crêpe batter is a thin pancake batter that is very easy to make. You can vary it by adding a bit of sugar, vanilla or grated orange peel for desserts (omit the pepper), or by adding finely chopped fresh herbs for savory crêpes. Make them ahead, stack them between pieces of waxed paper and freeze in a freezer bag.

You can also use this filling in tortilla rolls, or in little appetizer sandwiches made with very thinly sliced challah.

3 eggs
1 cup (250 mL) milk or soy milk
½ cup (125 mL) water
2 tbsp (25 mL) vegetable oil
¾ cup (175 mL) all-purpose flour
½ tsp (2 mL) kosher salt

FILLING
½ cup (125 mL) mayonnaise
2 tbsp (25 mL) sweet Russian-style mustard
12 oz (375 g) smoked salmon, thinly sliced
2 tbsp (25 mL) finely chopped preserved lemon peel,
    or 1 tbsp (15 mL) grated lemon peel
24 sprigs fresh dill or chives

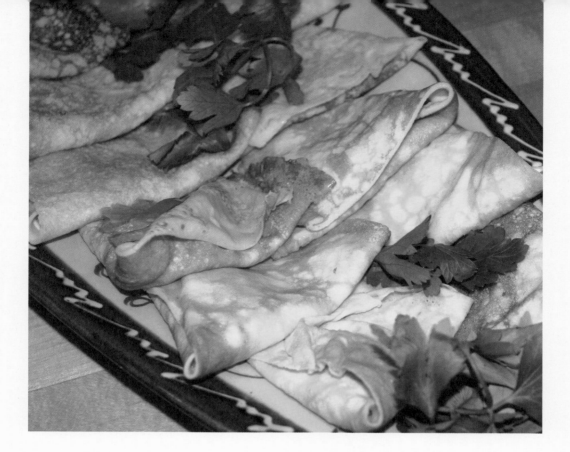

1. In a blender or food processor or with a whisk, combine eggs, milk, water, oil, flour and salt. Blend until smooth. Transfer batter to a bowl and cover. Let batter rest at room temperature for 30 minutes, or refrigerate for a few hours. (If batter thickens too much, thin with a little water. It should be the consistency of unwhipped whipping cream.)

2. To make crêpes, heat an 8- or 9-inch (20 or 23 cm) lightly oiled crêpe pan, omelet pan or nonstick skillet over medium heat. Pour in ¼ cup (50 mL) batter and swirl to coat bottom of pan. Cook for 1 to 2 minutes, or until browned. Flip and cook second side for 1 minute. Second side will not brown as nicely so always keep first side on the outside for the nicest appearance. Stack crêpes as they are made.

3. In a small bowl, combine mayonnaise and mustard. Taste and add more mustard if you wish.

4. Cut crêpes in half and spread with a thin layer of mustard mayonnaise. Place a slice or two of smoked salmon on mayo in a single layer. Sprinkle with lemon peel. Fold each crêpe in thirds (they will look like triangles). Place a sprig of dill or a chive in the last fold. Refrigerate until about 30 minutes before serving.

MAKES 20 TO 24 PIECES

Barbecued Chicken with Lemon Chipotle Baste

Everyone loves barbecued chicken, but it is one of the hardest things to cook without the outside burning and the inside being raw. Boneless, skinless breasts and thighs are delicious and cook very quickly, but when I want the added flavor of the skin and bones, I brown the chicken for about 5 minutes per side on the barbecue and then finish it on the cooler side of the grill or in a 400°F (200°C) oven.

LEMON CHIPOTLE BASTE
¼ cup (50 mL) extra-virgin olive oil or melted butter

¼ cup (50 mL) lemon juice

3 cloves garlic, minced

2 tbsp (25 mL) pureed chipotles

2 tbsp (25 mL) Worcestershire sauce

1 tbsp (15 mL) honey

1 tbsp (15 mL) fresh thyme, or 1 tsp (5 mL) dried

1 tsp (5 mL) kosher salt

CHICKEN
2 3-lb (1.5 kg) chickens, cut in quarters
   (or just breasts or thighs, bone in, skin on)

¼ cup (50 mL) extra-virgin olive oil

1 tbsp (15 mL) paprika

1 tbsp (15 mL) kosher salt

¼ tsp (1 mL) pepper

1. To prepare baste, in a bowl, combine oil, lemon juice, garlic, chipotles, Worcestershire, honey, thyme and salt.
2. Rub chicken with oil, paprika, salt and pepper. Grill for about 5 minutes per side, or until browned.
3. Transfer chicken, skin side up, to cooler part of grill and cook, with barbecue lid down, for 20 to 30 minutes, or until internal temperature reaches 165°F (75°C). Baste with lemon mixture every 10 minutes (I use a brush). (Or transfer browned chicken to a baking sheet and finish cooking in a preheated 400°F/200°C oven for 30 minutes.) Stop basting for last 5 minutes of cooking to make sure any uncooked chicken juices in basting sauce don't end up on chicken.

MAKES 8 SERVINGS

Coleslaw

For people who love a vinaigrette-style coleslaw, this is a great one. And it really cuts the richness of a barbecue meal (if you prefer a creamy coleslaw, use the creamy dressing below). When financial advisor Alex Beauregard (our part-time bartender) tasted this, he said it was even better than Swiss Chalet. Hmm. A compliment doesn't get much better than that!

> 1 small cabbage, shredded (about 4 cups / 1 L)
> 1 carrot, grated
> 3 green onions, finely chopped
>
> DRESSING
> ⅓ cup (75 mL) cider vinegar or rice vinegar
> 2 tbsp (25 mL) granulated sugar
> 1 tsp (5 mL) ground cumin (preferably toasted)
> ⅓ cup (75 mL) vegetable oil
> Salt and pepper to taste

1. Combine cabbage, carrot and green onions in a large bowl.
2. In a small saucepan, combine vinegar, sugar, cumin and oil and bring to a boil.
3. Add dressing to cabbage and toss. Season to taste with salt and pepper.

MAKES 8 SERVINGS

Creamy Coleslaw Dressing
In a small bowl, combine 1 minced garlic clove, 2 tbsp (25 mL) lime juice, 1 tsp (5 mL) ground cumin, ½ tsp (2 mL) hot red pepper sauce, 1 tbsp (15 mL) granulated sugar and 1 cup (250 mL) mayonnaise. Taste and adjust seasonings if necessary.
　　Makes about 1 cup (250 mL).

Moroccan Sweet Pepper and Bread Salad

This is like an Italian bread salad with Moroccan flavors. Argan oil is a delicious nutty, oil that is traditional in Morocco and becoming fashionable. If you can't find it, or if it is too expensive, just use walnut oil or additional olive oil.

½ Italian loaf or pita bread (about 8 oz/ 250 g)
2 tbsp (25 mL) extra-virgin olive oil
1 tsp (5 mL) kosher salt

DRESSING
1 clove garlic, peeled
1 tsp (5 mL) kosher salt
¼ tsp (1 mL) pepper
1 tsp (5 mL) ground cumin (preferably toasted)
2 plum tomatoes, peeled, seeded and cut in chunks
2 tbsp (25 mL) red wine vinegar or sherry vinegar
⅓ cup (75 mL) extra-virgin olive oil
¼ cup (50 mL) argan oil, walnut oil or extra-virgin olive oil

SALAD
4 sweet red peppers, roasted, peeled, seeded and diced
4 poblano peppers or green peppers, roasted, peeled, seeded and diced
2 cups (500 mL) cherry tomatoes, fresh or roasted (page 24)
½ cup (125 mL) chopped fresh cilantro
¼ cup (50 mL) chopped fresh parsley
1 cup (250 mL) pitted black olives

1. Break bread into 1½-inch (4 cm) chunks and toss with oil and salt on a baking sheet. Bake in a preheated 400°F (200°C) oven for 8 to 10 minutes, or until toasted but still chewy.
2. Meanwhile, to prepare dressing, combine garlic, salt, pepper, cumin, plum tomatoes, vinegar, olive oil and argan oil in a food processor and blend until smooth. Taste and adjust seasonings with salt, pepper or olive oil.
3. Toss bread, peppers, tomatoes, cilantro, parsley and olives with dressing.

MAKES 8 SERVINGS

Sweet Cornbread

Anthony Rose, executive chef of Toronto's Drake Hotel, cooked this—his favorite cornbread—in one of his classes at my school. Now it is our favorite, too. Reduce the amount of sugar if you prefer it less sweet.

This recipe makes a large cornbread. I like to freeze leftovers for stuffings (page 35) or croutons (page 127). Add diced olives, sun-dried tomatoes or fresh herbs if you wish.

> 2 cups (500 mL) all-purpose flour
> 1½ cups (375 mL) cornmeal
> 2 tbsp (25 mL) baking powder
> 1½ tsp (7 mL) kosher salt
> ½ cup (125 mL) granulated sugar
> 2 eggs
> ¼ cup (50 mL) extra-virgin olive oil or melted butter
> 2½ cups (625 mL) buttermilk or sour soy milk
> 1 cup (250 mL) corn kernels, grilled (page 252), optional
> 1 jalapeño, seeded and chopped, optional

1. In a large bowl, combine flour, cornmeal, baking powder, salt and sugar.
2. In a separate bowl, combine eggs, oil and buttermilk.
3. Add egg mixture to large bowl and combine. Add corn and jalapeño, if using. Stir until all ingredients are moistened.
4. Transfer batter to an oiled 13- x 9-inch (3 L) baking dish. Bake in a preheated 350°F (180°C) oven for 35 minutes, or until bread springs back when pressed in center or a cake tester comes out clean.
5. Cool for 20 minutes before cutting into wedges or squares.

MAKES ONE LARGE CORNBREAD

Sour Milk

To make sour milk or sour soy milk, place 1 tbsp (15 mL) lemon juice or plain vinegar in a measuring cup and add milk or soy milk to make 1 cup (250 mL). Allow to rest for 10 minutes before using (don't worry if milk looks curdled).

Makes 1 cup (250 mL).

Blueberry Cobbler

This cobbler has a wonderful buttermilk cakelike topping, and it comes from my good friend and fantastic baker Jim Dodge, considered to be one of the leading influences on contemporary American cuisine.

8 cups (2 L) fresh or frozen blueberries
⅓ cup (75 mL) granulated sugar
½ tsp (2 mL) ground cinnamon

TOPPING
½ cup (125 mL) butter or margarine
¾ cup (175 mL) granulated sugar
1 egg
1 tsp (5 mL) vanilla paste or pure vanilla extract
1⅓ cups (325 mL) all-purpose flour
1 tsp (5 mL) baking soda
½ tsp (2 mL) cream of tartar
¼ tsp (1 mL) kosher salt
¾ cup (175 mL) buttermilk or sour soy milk (page 278)
2 tbsp (25 mL) coarse sugar

1. In a large bowl, combine blueberries, sugar and cinnamon. Spoon into an oiled 13- x 9-inch (3 L) baking dish.
2. To prepare topping, in a large bowl, cream butter and sugar until light. Beat in egg and vanilla.
3. In a separate bowl, combine flour, baking soda, cream of tartar and salt.
4. Add dry ingredients to butter mixture alternately with buttermilk in three additions, ending with flour.
5. Spoon batter on top of blueberries, leaving a space around edge so fruit juices can bubble up. (Drop batter rather than spreading it so blueberries do not get mixed into batter at all.) Sprinkle with coarse sugar.
6. Bake in a preheated 350°F (180°C) oven for 40 to 45 minutes, or until topping is cooked through and browned, and fruit is juicy and bubbling on sides.

MAKES 8 SERVINGS

STRAWBERRY LIME SANGRIA

GRILLED PIZZA WITH CARAMELIZED ONIONS AND CHEDDAR

GRILLED TUNA WITH SALSA VERDE

BUTTERNUT AND BOCCONCINI SALAD

HEIRLOOM TOMATO SALAD WITH BALSAMIC

THANK GOODNESS IT'S THE WEEKEND CHOCOLATE CREAM PIE

al fresco dinner

SERVES 8

Whoever said that food tastes better outside had a point. In Canada, summer is so short that we have to take advantage of nice weather. It doesn't have to be a picnic—even Canadians are buying into outdoor kitchens, restaurants are adding patios wherever possible, and al fresco dinners are becoming more and more popular.

Many parts of this menu can be prepared ahead, but finish the pizzas in the oven, toss the salad, add the sparkling wine to the sangria and grill the tuna just before serving. For an even easier appetizer, try the Brie with Caramelized Onions (page 287).

Strawberry Lime Sangria

This is so refreshing. The non-alcoholic Bacardi margarita mixer is a pretty good substitute for lime juice and sugar and a much better choice than that bright green frozen limeade. You can use frozen or fresh berries—the frozen can always be on hand, and they don't need to be washed!

For a non-alcoholic version, add ginger ale or sparkling water instead of the wine.

4 cups (1 L) fresh or frozen strawberries
2 cups (500 mL) frozen Bacardi margarita mixer,
   or 1 cup (250 mL) lime juice and 1 cup (250 mL) sugar syrup (page 86)
3 cups (750 mL) sparkling white wine (e.g., Prosecco or Cava)
Ice cubes

1. In a blender or food processor, puree berries and margarita mixer until smooth. Refrigerate.
2. Add sparkling wine just before serving. Serve over ice.

MAKES 8 SERVINGS

Strawberry Lime Martinis
Add 1½ cups (375 mL) vodka or rum instead of sparkling wine.

Grilled Pizza with Caramelized Onions and Cheddar

It is hard to imagine grilling pizza dough, but it really does work brilliantly. Even the grilled crust on its own tastes fantastic. You can buy the dough instead of making it and use any kind of cheese. Roasted cherry tomatoes (page 24) also make a great topping.

I usually make a triple batch of caramelized onions and freeze them in 1-cup (250 mL) portions. That way I have them on hand to use on pizzas, pierogi (page 90) or quiche (pages 170–171) whenever I want.

I like to grill the crust ahead and then finish the pizza in the oven, but you can also finish it on the barbecue. Reduce the heat to low when you turn the crust, add the topping, close the lid and grill it for 4 to 5 minutes, or until the cheese melts.

CRUST

1 cup (250 mL) warm water

1 tbsp (15 mL) granulated sugar

1 tbsp (15 mL) dry yeast (1 package)

3 cups (750 mL) all-purpose flour (or half whole wheat), approx.

1 tsp (5 mL) kosher salt

2 tbsp (25 mL) extra-virgin olive oil, divided

TOPPING

2 tbsp (25 mL) extra-virgin olive oil

3 large onions, thinly sliced

1 tbsp (15 mL) brown sugar

1 tbsp (15 mL) balsamic vinegar

12 oz (375 g) smoked Cheddar cheese, grated (3 cups/750 mL)

2 tbsp (25 mL) chopped fresh tarragon

1. To prepare crust, combine warm water and sugar in a large bowl. Sprinkle with yeast. Let stand for 10 minutes, or until yeast bubbles up.
2. Stir in about 1½ cups (375 mL) flour, salt and 1 tbsp (15 mL) oil. This can be done by hand, in a mixer or in a food processor. Continue to add flour until dough is still very soft but does not stick to your fingers too badly.
3. Knead dough for 5 to 8 minutes, or until smooth. Form into a ball and place in a large bowl with remaining 1 tbsp (15 mL) oil. Roll dough in oil. Cover and let rise for 1 to 1½ hours, or until dough doubles in volume.
4. Punch dough down and divide into 8 pieces. Roll or stretch out thinly. Do not worry if crusts are uneven in shape. Brush both sides with extra oil.
5. Grill crusts for 1 minute per side. Place grilled crusts in a single layer on baking sheets. (This can be done ahead.)
6. Meanwhile, to caramelize onions, heat oil in a large skillet over medium heat. Add onions and cook gently for a few minutes until lightly browned. Add sugar and balsamic and cook for about 20 minutes, or until well browned. Cool.
7. Top pizza crusts with onions, cheese and tarragon.
8. Bake pizzas in a preheated 400°F (200°C) oven for 10 to 12 minutes, or until cheese bubbles.

MAKES 8 INDIVIDUAL PIZZAS

Brie with Caramelized Onions

Elizabeth Pizzinato has a huge holiday party every December. She has great recipes for all kinds of appetizers, and this one is really fantastic.

Heat 2 tbsp (25 mL) butter in a large, deep skillet over medium-high heat. Add 4 chopped onions and cook for 20 to 25 minutes, or until tender and brown.

Add 2 finely chopped garlic cloves and sprinkle with 2 tbsp (25 mL) granulated sugar and 1 tbsp (15 mL) fresh thyme. Cook for a few minutes. Add ¼ cup (50 mL) dry white wine and cook for 10 minutes longer. Season with salt and pepper to taste.

Unwrap an 8-inch (20 cm) round of Brie or Camembert (about 2 lb/1 kg), cut off and discard top crust and return cheese to wooden box (or wrap cheese well in foil, leaving top exposed. Spread with onions and place on a parchment-lined baking sheet.

Bake in a preheated 350°F (180°C) oven for 20 to 25 minutes, or until Brie just starts to melt. Serve cheese in box, accompanied by crackers and bread.

Makes 8 to 12 servings.

Grilled Tuna with Salsa Verde

Many people want to eat more fish, but they want it to be like meat. Fresh tuna looks like steak and tastes so meaty that even confirmed meat-lovers like it. Just be sure not to overcook it; it should be rare in the center, just like a rare steak (which is great with this salsa verde, too).

SALSA VERDE

2 cups (500 mL) packed fresh parsley
¼ cup (50 mL) fresh mint
2 anchovies, rinsed, or 1 tbsp (15 mL) anchovy paste
1 tbsp (15 mL) capers, rinsed and drained
1 clove garlic, peeled
1 tsp (5 mL) Dijon mustard
1 tbsp (15 mL) red wine vinegar
1 tbsp (15 mL) lemon juice
½ cup (125 mL) extra-virgin olive oil

TUNA

1 2-lb (1 kg) tuna steak, about 1 inch (2.5 cm) thick
2 tbsp (25 mL) extra-virgin olive oil
1 tbsp (15 mL) sea salt (e.g., Maldon)
1 tbsp (15 mL) coarsely ground pepper
2 bunches arugula or baby spinach, trimmed

1. To prepare salsa verde, chop parsley, mint, anchovies, capers and garlic in a food processor until fine. Add mustard, vinegar, lemon juice and oil. Blend into a rough paste by chopping on/off. Taste and add salt only if necessary (anchovies are salty).
2. To prepare fish, brush tuna with oil and sprinkle both sides with salt and pepper.
3. Grill tuna for about 2 minutes per side. It should still be rare in center. Slice and serve on a bed of arugula. Spoon salsa verde over tuna.

MAKES 8 SERVINGS

Butternut and Bocconcini Salad

Pumpkins and pumpkin seed oil are quickly gaining popularity. Pumpkins, with their bright color, vitamins and antioxidants, are very healthful, and dark greeny-brown pumpkin seed oil is nutty and delicious.

If you don't want to make the brittle, just sprinkle the salad with toasted salted pumpkin seeds or walnuts.

I don't usually peel the squash, but you can if you wish.

SQUASH
2 lb (1 kg) butternut squash, halved, seeded and cut in wedges
2 tbsp (25 mL) extra-virgin olive oil
1 tsp (5 mL) kosher salt
1 tbsp (15 mL) fresh thyme

DRESSING
2 tbsp (25 mL) balsamic vinegar
2 tbsp (25 mL) Port
1 tsp (5 mL) Dijon mustard
1 small clove garlic, minced
1 tsp (5 mL) kosher salt
¼ tsp (1 mL) pepper
⅓ cup (75 mL) extra-virgin olive oil
¼ cup (50 mL) pumpkin seed oil or extra-virgin olive oil

SALAD
12 cups (3 L) mixed salad greens or baby spinach
8 oz (250 g) bocconcini cheese, drained and broken in chunks
2 tbsp (25 mL) shredded fresh sage
1 cup (250 mL) pumpkin seed praline, optional

1. Arrange squash, skin side down, on a baking sheet. Drizzle or brush with olive oil and sprinkle with salt and thyme. Roast in a preheated 400°F (200°C) oven for about 30 minutes, or until tender and browned.
2. To prepare dressing, in a bowl, whisk together vinegar, Port, mustard, garlic, salt, pepper, olive oil and pumpkin seed oil.
3. Place greens in a large shallow bowl. Toss with dressing and top with squash, cheese, sage and praline, if using.

MAKES 8 SERVINGS

Pumpkin Seed Brittle

This delicious brittle is great on salads or for snacks.

In a saucepan, combine 1¼ cups (300 mL) brown sugar, ½ cup (125 mL) butter and 2 tbsp (25 mL) water. Bring to a boil and cook, stirring often, for 7 to 8 minutes, or until mixture reaches soft crack stage (when a spoonful of hot syrup is dropped in a bowl of very cold water, it should form firm but pliable threads when pulled apart) or 270°F (132°C).

Quickly stir in 1 tsp (5 mL) sea salt, ½ tsp (2 mL) toasted cumin seeds, ¼ tsp (1 mL) baking soda and 1½ cups (375 mL) pumpkin seeds. Immediately spread on a well-buttered baking sheet to form a 13- x 9-inch (33 x 23 cm) rectangle.

Refirgerate for 1 hour, or until set. Break or cut into irregular pieces.

Heirloom Tomato Salad with Balsamic

This is the easiest salad to make, but you have to use the best ingredients, including the freshest tomatoes. David Cohlmeyer of Cookstown Greens in Toronto, for example, grows wonderful heirloom tomatoes. They come in green, purple, yellow, orange and red, in all kinds of sizes and shapes, and they taste amazing.

Use the best balsamic vinegar you can afford, and use only extra-virgin olive oil, sea salt (I like Maldon) and freshly ground black pepper.

2 lb (1 kg) heirloom tomatoes
2 cups (500 mL) cherry tomatoes
3 tbsp (45 mL) aged balsamic vinegar
3 tbsp (45 mL) extra-virgin olive oil
Sea salt (e.g., Maldon) and freshly ground black pepper to taste
2 tbsp (25 mL) torn fresh basil

1. Slice heirloom tomatoes and place in a shallow dish. Sprinkle with cherry tomatoes.
2. Sprinkle tomatoes with vinegar, oil, salt, pepper and basil.

MAKES 8 SERVINGS

Thank Goodness It's the Weekend
Chocolate Cream Pie

We named this pie after seeing the film *Waitress*, where all the pies have wacky names.

For this pie you bake the pastry "blind" before adding the chocolate cream. If the pastry and filling are cold when the pie is put together, the bottom crust will not get too soggy. Another trick is to brush the cooked bottom crust with melted chocolate before adding the filling.

PASTRY

1 cup (250 mL) all-purpose flour
Pinch kosher salt
½ cup (125 mL) butter, cold, cut in pieces
3 tbsp (45 mL) ice water

FILLING

2½ cups (625 mL) milk, divided
¾ cup (175 mL) granulated sugar
¼ cup (50 mL) cornstarch
2 tbsp (25 mL) cocoa powder
2 eggs
8 oz (250 g) semisweet or bittersweet chocolate, chopped
2 tbsp (25 mL) butter
1 tbsp (15 mL) vanilla paste or pure vanilla extract

TOPPING

1 cup (250 mL) whipping cream
1 tbsp (15 mL) vanilla paste, or 1 tsp (5 mL) pure vanilla extract
   and 1 tbsp (15 mL) icing sugar

1. In a bowl, combine flour and salt. Cut butter into flour with fingertips or a pastry blender until it is in tiny bits. Sprinkle with ice water and gather into a ball. Knead lightly. Wrap in plastic wrap and refrigerate for 30 minutes.

2. On a floured surface, roll dough out into a 12-inch (30 cm) circle. Transfer to a 9-inch (23 cm) pie dish. Flute edge. Line crust with parchment paper and fill with dry beans, rice or clean pennies.

3. Bake in a preheated 425°F (220°C) oven for 15 minutes. Remove beans and paper. Return crust to oven. Reduce heat to 350°F (180°C) and continue to bake for 15 to 20 minutes, or until browned. Cool completely.

4. To prepare filling, heat 2 cups (500 mL) milk in a large saucepan over medium heat.

5. In a bowl, combine granulated sugar, cornstarch and cocoa. Whisk in remaining ½ cup (125 mL) cold milk. Beat in eggs.

6. Add hot milk to bowl slowly, whisking constantly. Return everything to saucepan and bring to a boil. Reduce heat and cook, stirring, for 2 minutes, or until thick.

7. Place chocolate and butter in a separate bowl and strain hot thick milk mixture into it. Stir until chocolate melts and mixture is smooth. Stir in vanilla. Place plastic wrap directly on surface of filling to prevent a skin from forming, and cool completely.

8. Spread cold chocolate mixture in baked pie crust.

9. To prepare topping, in a bowl, whip cream until light. Beat in vanilla paste and continue to beat until stiff. Spread over chocolate filling. Refrigerate for at least 1 hour before serving.

MAKES 8 TO 10 SERVINGS

index